P9-AOT-215

147 Fun Things To Do In HOUSTON

Third Millennium Edition

N2·FUN

written by
KAREN FOULK
illustrated by Annette Hruska

INTO FUN, COMPANY
PUBLICATIONS
A Division of Into Fun, Inc.
Sugar Land, Texas

147 Fun Things To Do In Houston
Third Edition
by Karen Foulk

Cover and Map illustrations by Annette Hruska
Cover, Map & Book Layout designed by Mark Thogersen

Copyright © 1997, 1998, 2000 Karen Foulk
First Edition, 1997
Second Printing of First Edition, August 1997
Second Edition with Coupons, 1998

Library of Congress
Catalog Card Number:
96-76785

ISBN 0-9652464-5-0

INTO FUN, COMPANY PUBLICATIONS
A Division of Into Fun, Inc.
P.O. Box 2494
Sugar Land, Texas 77487-2492

Printed & bound in the
United States of America

Into Fun, Co. Publications are available for
educational, business, and sales promotional use.
Please contact:
INTO FUN, INC.
P.O. Box 2494, Sugar Land, Texas 77479
Phone: 281-980-9745 Fax: 281-494-9745

With all my love,
To my husband, Don,
whom I have trouble
convincing that I am working.

Michael
Rachel
David
Rebecca

Acknowledgments

This work came about with the support and help
of many great friends and family members.

To my husband and children,
who probably initiated all this.

A special thanks to Annette Hruska, who from the
beginning caught the vision of this project and
persisted with her wonderful ideas.

To Barbara Harris, my dearest friend and
neighbor, who never let me give up.

To Sharon Cooper, for her famous words,
"Is it a book yet?"

To Merrill Littlewood, CPA. He's the best.

To Brocky Brown of Brockton Publishing Co. Inc.
for his cheering me through new adventures.

To Ken Barrow, for his support, ideas,
and legal advice.

To my sister, Jerrie Hurd;
this must be in our blood.

Table of Contents

This book contains descriptions including operating times and admission costs of many of the fun and interesting places in the Houston area. Although a great deal of effort has gone into making this book as up-to-date and accurate as possible, changes constantly occur. Therefore, before visiting a destination, please call to confirm the information provided herein. Neither Into Fun, Co. Publications, a division of Into Fun, Inc., the owner, nor the author warrant the accuracy of the information in this book which includes but is not limited to price changes, addresses, names, hours of operation, management or conditions of the attraction described.

Karen Foulk

I truly enjoyed putting this book together. In fact it's been so much fun, I have trouble convincing my husband that I'm working.

I wrote this book with your family in mind. Everything you need to know about Houston is at your fingertips. And this new edition's loaded. Be prepared to shop 'til you drop, eat lots of tasty food, and do tons of fun things. I love seeing families out-and-about having fun. Know a new family moving to Houston? Welcome them with this book.

Discover what's in your own backyard. With this updated edition, plan to see Houston as never before. Ever hear of the Radio Music Theater? Talk about fun! Here's one of my favorite places to go. These talented folks — three of them, playing multiple characters — put on great show. If you go, plan for your whole family to laugh themselves sick.

Eating out in Houston's a treat. We have wonderful restaurants, many with ethnic foods from around the world. Eating here's like visiting many other countries without the airfares. I've listed restaurants with fantastic English, Lebanese, Vietnamese, French, Thai, Persian, and Indian cuisine. But then, there's no place like home — you must try the Texas barbecue places that I've mentioned. Oh and then there's the Cheesecake Factory!

Not everything I list is in Houston. I tell you of places I think every Houston family should know about. Canoeing in the Big Thicket in Kountz, Texas is fun, fun, fun — take the kids. Or riding the vintage train in Rusk — take the kids. Impress your out-of-town guests and relatives with an alligator-infested swamp tour in Orange — and take the kids. Places like these I want to share with you.

My book's small, so it can fit into the glove compartment of your car. It fits in mom's purse, too. The idea is to never be without it.

Now a word about my books, I update them regularly and write new ones constantly. Keep up with me — watch for my new books on other cities. Really experience the Texas coast, San Antonio, or New Orleans — and soon Dallas, Austin, and the Hill Country. You'll visit new places like a pro. Simply let my guidebooks do all the work for you.

Build lots of fun, memorable experiences with your family in Houston.

Karen Foulk

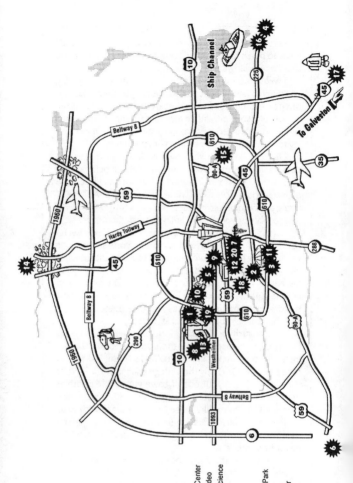

Locations

1. Americas Restaurant
2. Astrodome Tour
3. AstroWorld/WaterWorld
4. Battleship *Texas*
5. Bayou Bend Gardens
6. Brazos Bend State Park
7. Burke Baker Planetarium
8. The Galleria
9. Hard Rock Cafe
10. Houston Arboretum & Nature Center
11. Houston Livestock Show & Rodeo
12. Houston Museum of Natural Science
13. Ice Skating at the Galleria
14. Old Town Spring
15. Port of Houston Tour
16. San Jacinto Monument State Park
17. Space Center Houston
18. The Texas Medical Center Tour
19. Transco Tower
20. Wortham IMAX Theater

Chapter 1
WHAT'S HOUSTON GOT TO SHOW OFF?

AMERICAS RESTAURANT

1800 Post Oak, Houston

713-961-1492

(note the "1492" phone number)

A restaurant featuring cuisines from the Americas

One of those places Houston is proud to have. Opened in 1993. Chosen by Esquire Magazine as the "best new restaurant in the country."

Foods cooked are native to this hemisphere. Cooking styles are influenced by North, South, and Central American cultures, such as Peruvian, Argentinean, Southwestern, Spanish, French, and Mexican.

Hours

Mon - Thurs	11:30 am - 10 pm
Friday	11:30 am - 11 pm
Saturday	5 pm - 11 pm
Sunday	Closed

Call for reservations.

Cost

Moderate to expensive

One-of-a-kind special dining experience. Dressy. Great place to take out-of-town guests and relatives. Take husbands, wives, dates, or friends for lunch.

Directions

From the 610 West Loop exit Westheimer and go west. Turn right on Post Oak. Located in the Saks Fifth Avenue Pavilion.

ASTRODOME USA TOUR

610 South at Kirby
713-799-9595

A tour of Houston's domed stadium

First domed stadium ever, with seats for 55,000 baseball, 62,000 for football. Home of the ASTROS. Visit the press seats, the sky boxes, and walk on the astroturf. Watch a 16-minute movie explaining how it was built. Known as the "8th Wonder."

Tour Hours

For walk-in guests
Tues. - Sat.: 11 am, 1 pm
Group Tours (Reservations in advance)

Cost for Individuals

Children under 3 . . . . Free
Children ages 4-11 . . . . $3
Adults $4
Seniors (65+) $3

Cost for Group Tours (per adult)

10-19 Adults $4
20-30 Adults $3
31 or more Adults $2.75

Cost for Group Tours (per child)

10-19 Children $3
20-30 Children $2.50
31 or more Children $2

Parking costs $5

Tour lasts 1 hour and 15 minutes.

No charge for adults or chaperones accompanying childrens groups.

Directions

Located on the 610 South Loop. Exit Kirby. Enter west gate #2.

ASTROWORLD/ WATERWORLD

9001 Kirby Drive
713-799-1234

A Six Flags Amusement Park

Over a hundred rides and shows, plus a water park. Something for all ages. Very clean, security minded, well operated. It's a great place to take the family.

Hours
Seasonal

Cost

Children under 2	Free
Children under 48 inches	$16.50
Adults & Children over 48"	$32.99
Seniors (55 and older)	$21.99
Parking	$5

Enough can't be said for "Season Passes." Bought conveniently at Kroger, they make the park a bargain. Individual passes are $64.99. Get your pass before April and a season pass to WaterWorld is included for the same price.

Watch for special holiday activities at the Park such as "Fright Night" around Halloween. The Southern Star Amphitheater offers good entertainment (Call the Six Flags concert line at 713-799-1234).

note: lockers and strollers available. Food inside the park is expensive and outside food is not allowed in. You can leave the park to eat sandwiches from a cooler in your car or drive to a local restaurant before returning.

Directions
Located on the 610 South Loop. Take the Kirby exit.

BATTLESHIP TEXAS

3527 Battleground Rd, La Porte TX
281-479-2411

The kids will enjoy exploring this old battleship

Travel in time back to WORLD WAR I and II days—battles fought, victories won. Having survived both wars, she was powerful in her day. See why Texas is proud of her. Interesting. Educational. Take family and guests.

Hours

Daily .... 10 am - 5 pm
(except some holidays)

Cost

Children under 6 .... Free
Children ages 6-18 .... $2.50
Adults $5
Seniors $3

Simple to tour. Follow the marked tour path. Note: lots of walking and climbing. Wear comfortable shoes. Small children must be supervised. Recently improved and further restored. Beautiful. Close to the San Jacinto Monument.

Directions

Located 21 miles east of downtown Houston next to the San Jacinto Monument. From the 610 East Loop exit Highway 225 and go east. Exit #134 (San Jacinto Monument and Museum) and go north. Follow 3 miles to the Monument. Watch for signs.

BAYOU BEND GARDENS

I Westcott
713-639-7750

One of the most beautiful places in Houston

Walk the grounds of the Hogg Estate with 14 acres of gardens maintained by the River Oaks Garden Club. Also a part of the Azalea Trail held each March. The most impressive time to see the gardens is when the azaleas are in bloom.

One of our finest American art collections in the Hogg Home. (Part of the Museum of Fine Arts). See page on the Bayou Bend Museum.

A must-see. Paths are easy to follow. Plan to take your time. Great place to take any out-of-town guest, grandparent, or family member. Wear comfortable shoes.

Hours

Closed Monday

Tues - Sat . . . . 10 am - 5 pm
Sunday . . . . 1 pm - 5 pm

Cost

Adults $3
Children under 10 . . . . Free
Every third Sunday of each month: Free

Directions

From the 610 West Loop, exit Memorial Drive. Go east. Turn south at Westcott and proceed to the parking lot. Cross the footbridge to the grounds.

BRAZOS BEND STATE PARK

21901 FM 762, Needville TX
409-553-5101

One of Houston's best places to go

Wonderful place for any out-of-town guest who simply must see an alligator. Picnic under huge moss-draped live oaks. Walk numerous trails along marshes and observe the wildlife. Great facilities for a day trip or spend the night. Campsites available but check first as they fill up sometimes. Fishing allowed. Places to bicycle. Grills for outdoor cooking.

Hours

Weekdays (the park) ..... 8 am - 10 pm
Fri, Sat, & Sun .... 7 am - 10 pm
Office Hours Daily .... 8 am - 5 pm
For camping reservations call 512-389-8900
Monday through Friday ..... 8 am - 6 pm.

Cost

Age 12 & under .... Free
Age 13-65 .... $3 per person

Keep your pet on a leash. Beautiful any time of the year. One of Houston's best places to go. A must-see. Don't forget the camera. Also offering the George Observatory and the Challenger Learning Center.

State Park Directions

Located approximately one hour southwest of downtown Houston. Take the 59 Freeway south across the Brazos River to the Brazos Bend State Park/Grand Parkway exit. Go left over the freeway and follow FM762 for approximately 20 miles. Watch for signs.

BURKE BAKER PLANETARIUM

1 Hermann Circle Drive
713-639-IMAX (4629)

Houston's Planetarium Shows have a lot to offer

Seats recline. Stars appear. Discoveries of the universe are explained. Interesting, educational shows. Newly renovated; a must-see. Impress your children. Popular program during the week for school groups. Worth seeing. Variety of shows for weekends. Watch for their Christmas special. Shows generally last 30-45 minutes. Weekend evenings cater to the teen-age crowd with "Laser Rock" shows. Children under 3 are not admitted to Planetarium Shows except for children's shows.

Hours: Show times vary, must call for information.

Cost

Children ages 3 - 11	$3
Adults	$4
Members	$2.50
Seniors	$3
Groups of 20+ (per person)	$1.50

Cost for Laser Rock Shows

Teenagers (12+) & Adults	$6
Members	$3
Seniors	$6
Groups of 20+ (per person)	$6

Located inside the Museum of Natural Science.
Other attractions in Hermann Park may impact parking.

Directions

If you are coming south on Hwy 59: Exit Fanin and continue south on Fanin. Stay in second lane from left. This will bring you to Hermann Park. The Museum is the first building on your left as you enter the park.

If you are coming north on Hwy 59: Exit Richmond and continue east on Richmond. Turn right at second light onto Fannin and continue south on Fannin. Stay in second lane from left. This will bring you to Hermann Park. The Museum is the first building on your left as you enter the park.

THE GALLERIA

5015 Westheimer
713-622-0663

The ultimate place to shop

Walk the shops that are barely affordable. Finest in fashion, gifts, and wares. See what's in and new. Great eateries.

Famous to Houston. Great place to take out-of-town guests you may want to impress. Huge public ice skating rink. Greatest place in town to visit Santa during the holidays.

Hours

Mon - Sat .... 10 am - 9 pm
Sunday .... Noon to 6 pm

Expensive but great sales. Plan to spend the day. Entrance #1 on Westheimer takes you to the main section near the elevators. Free parking almost everywhere including the underground garage. Security 24 hours a day.

Directions

Located east of 610 West Loop on Westheimer. From the 610 West Loop, exit Westheimer and go west. Will be down one block on the left.

What's Houston Got To Show Off?

HARD ROCK CAFE

2801 Kirby (near Westheimer) 77098
713-520-1134
www.hardrock.com

A place with great food, fun atmosphere, and famous collectibles

Memorabilia from early rock 'n' roll days to present. Hundreds of rock stars' guitars, a 1958 Harley, and numerous gold albums. Great atmosphere. Fun. Try the watermelon ribs and hickory barbecue chicken combo.

Different kinds of burgers, wonderful desserts. Take the kids one afternoon. A must for the out-of-town teen guest whose hard rock collection may include: Aspen, Las Vegas, New York, New Orleans, Singapore, Tel Aviv, Maui, Sydney, San Francisco, Chicago ... and now Houston. There are 44 Hard Rock Cafes in the United States and 98 world wide.

T-shirts aren't the only thing to buy. New collectibles include watches, pins, teddy bears, hats, mugs, jackets, and more.

Hours

Fri - Sat	11 am - 11:30 pm
Bar	open until 11:30 pm
Sun - Thurs	11 am - 10:30 pm
Bar	open until 10 pm

Cost

Moderatly Priced

Look for Sally, their famous Thunderbird, atop a 30 foot tower.

Directions

From the 59 Freeway, exit on Kirby and go north.
Go two lights and it will be on the right.

18

HOUSTON ARBORETUM AND NATURE CENTER

4501 Woodway
713-681-8433

A wonderful place for the family to enjoy the great outdoors

Imagine enjoying and learning about nature in urban Houston. This wildlife sanctuary of 155 acres is located by Memorial Park. Classes offered on Saturdays for kids ages 5-12 are very popular. Must sign up early.

A mixture of hardwood and pine trees, ponds, wild flowers. Over five miles of trails. Wear tennis shoes and comfortable clothes. Great activity for the whole family, out-of-town guests, and relatives. Visit the Discovery Room and gift shop.

Hours

Daily . . . . 8:30 am - 6 pm
Discovery Room . . . . 10 am - 4 pm
The Discovery Room is closed on Monday

Cost

Free

Directions

Located by Memorial Park, 2/10 mile east of the 610 West Loop. Take the Woodway exit from the 610 West Loop. Go east. Get in the right hand lane and watch for sign. Arboretum will be shortly on the right.

HOUSTON LIVESTOCK SHOW AND RODEO

Astrodome
610 South at Kirby
713-791-9000

The #1 biggest event in Houston

The world's largest rodeo! Held each year in February. Grab your hat and boots. Houston goes Western. Trail riders in covered wagons and on horseback tie up traffic as they come into town. School children and places of business dress up. All-time favorite country western singers conclude each evening's rodeo. Attend the livestock show. See the judging of this year's champions. Wonderful booths with crafts and wares. Have your children's pictures taken on the bull. All of this is in the Astrodome Complex.

Avoid the traffic problems and arrive early. Livestock show opens at 10 am. Rest rooms can be difficult to locate.

Lots of walking, wear comfortable shoes. Strollers come in handy when small children tire. Be prepared to smell like the animals. Leave a towel in the car to wipe off shoes.

Cost

Admission for Livestock Show & Rodeo
All day (including concerts) $12
Children under 3 . . . . Free

All day Admission for Livestock Show & Carnival
Adults $5
Children 6-12 (under 5 free) $2
(Watch for rodeo ticket sales. Tickets can be purchased through Ticket Master.)

Directions

Located in the Astrodome. Exit Kirby from the 610 South Loop. Parking is $5.

20

HOUSTON MUSEUM OF NATURAL SCIENCE

1 Hermann Circle Dr.

713-639-4600

One of Houston's finest museums

Seventy-foot, one hundred forty million year old Diplodocus dinosaur on display along with 400 other specimens in a new permanent exhibit that opened May 1994. See the six-million-dollar gem and mineral collection. Over 2,500 shells. Now opening is the new electrifying Wiess Energy Hall that explores the role of the earth sciences in the oil and natural gas industries. Take the entire family. A must-see. Also relax in the IMAX theater, gaze at the out-of-this-world Burke Baker Planetarium and hike through the three-level live Butterfly Center—all under one roof!

Hours

Mon - Sat	9 am - 6 pm
Sunday	11 am - 6 pm

Cost for Museum

Children ages 3-11	$3
Adults	$4 5
Seniors & Groups of 20+ (per person)	$3
Members	Free

Cost for Butterfly Center

$12 china

Children ages 3-11	$3
Adults	$4
Members	$2.50
Groups of 20+ (per person)	$1.50

Tuesday from 2 pm - 6 pm (8 pm in the summer), admission is free. Watch newspapers for interesting visiting exhibits. Two great gift shops with unique, educational items. You'll want to spend time browsing. McDonalds is open inside the museum. NOTE: Family memberships do save.

Directions

See directions to Burke Baker Planetarium (page 16).

ICE SKATING
AT THE GALLERIA

5015 Westheimer
713-621-1500

A fantastic place to go ice skating

Tired of the heat and humidity? Escape. Go ice skating. Centered in Houston's famous Galleria Mall. Open daily for public skating. One of the finest rinks. Private/group lessons as well as discount packages available.

Hours

Call before you go, times vary

Mon	9 am - 4 pm/8 -10 pm
Tues	9 am - 5 pm/8 -10 pm
Wed & Thurs	9 am - 4 pm/8 -10 pm
Friday	9 am - 11 pm
Saturday	Noon - 11 pm
Sunday	Noon - 6 pm

Cost

Children & Adults	$5/Session
Skate Rental	$2.50

Also a delightful way to usher in the Christmas spirit and see the Galleria gorgeously decorated for the holidays. We recommend seeing Santa here.

Directions

Located inside the Galleria. From the 610 West Loop exit Westheimer and go west. Will be down a few blocks on the left.

OLD TOWN SPRING

123-E Midway, Spring, Texas
281-353-9310 or 800-OLD TOWN

Hundreds of unique shops

Fantastic place for any mother-in-law who needs impressing. Get the girlfriends together. Plan to spend the entire day. Over a hundred unique shops with turn-of-the-century Texas small town charm. Offers a variety of unique things like antiques, crafts, collectibles, fine imported items. Lots of things for the home. Great places to lunch.

Open All Year! - Shop Hours

Tues - Sat . . . . 10 am - 5 pm
Sunday . . . . Noon - 5 pm
(Some shops are open on Monday)

Prices range from reasonable to expensive. A difficult place to push a stroller. Wear comfortable shoes. Caution to parents: stores are cluttered. Things in easy reach of small children.

To usher in the holiday spirit, Old Town Spring has an open house two weekends in November. A family event. See the splendidly decorated shops and dressed-up shopkeepers. Also, every April or May is their Crawfish Festival, a must-do.

Directions

Take I-45 North about ten miles north of Beltway 8. Take the Spring Cypress exit. Go east one mile. You can't miss it.

PORT OF HOUSTON TOUR

7300 Clinton at Gate #8
713-670-2416

A tour of the Houston Ship Channel

Cruise the Houston Ship Channel for free. See what has grown from modest beginnings to the third largest port in our country. Did you know that each year port activities have a three-billion-dollar impact on our area's economy? Air-conditioned, clean, comfortable leather seats. You will enjoy every minute aboard the "SAM HOUSTON." This is a 90-minute tour. A must-see. Tours by reservations only. Make reservations well in advance. This is a popular attraction.

Tour Hours

Tue, Wed, Fri, & Sat .... 10 am & 2:30 pm
Thurs and Sun .... 2:30 pm
(Does not operate Mondays and Holidays)

Reservation Office Hours

(Closed between 12:30 -1:30)
Mon - Fri .... 8:30 am - 5:30 pm

Cost

Free

Guide tells you about points of interest over the speaker. A million-dollar Pavilion. Note: Tuesdays, Wednesdays, and Thursdays are better days to see more activity on the ship channel. Weekends tend to be quieter.

Directions

Take 610 East Loop to Clinton Drive. Exit and go toward town (west) approximately 2 miles. Watch for signs for Gate #8 on the left.

SAN JACINTO MONUMENT & BATTLEGROUND STATE HISTORICAL PARK

One Monument Circle, La Porte, TX 77571
281-479-2421

See Texas history at its finest

Five hundred seventy feet high, taller than the Washington Monument. See how things really are bigger in Texas! Dedicated battleground. Sacred. Deserving every bit as much attention as the famous Alamo. Taking the Mexican Army totally by surprise, this battle lasted less than twenty minutes, securing our independence. Note the use of native limestone with its many fossils. You'll find the observation deck a high point in more ways than one. On clear days, the view is spectacular. Observe the activity on the ship channel.

Elevator Hours

Daily .... 9 am - 6 pm

Cost For Elevator Ride

Children under 11 .... $2.50
Adults $3
Seniors (65+) $2.50

See the museum free, with its priceless artifacts. Excellent displays. Will interest everyone. Even the youngest will love the gun display. Also see the gift shop. Great for Texas memorabilia. See *Texas Forever,* a 35-minute film.

Museum Hours

Daily .... 9 am - 6 pm

Directions

Located 21 miles east of downtown Houston. From the 610 East Loop exit Highway 225. Exit 134 (San Jacinto Monument and Museum) and go north. Follow 3 miles to the Monument. Watch for signs.

SPACE CENTER HOUSTON

1601 NASA Road 1, Clear Lake TX 77058
281-244-2100 • 800-972-0369

Visit NASA in a new way

See NASA's Space Center. This $70 million facility opened Fall of 1992. Designed by Disney with lots of high tech. See great IMAX features, too. Learn how astronauts live in space. Climb aboard a mock-up space shuttle. See how space exploration has evolved over the years. Best of all, actually see astronauts training for future missions. You will leave with a great appreciation for our space exploration program. Kids Space Center is a must-see.

Hours

Winter Weekdays	10 am - 5 pm
Sat - Sun	10 am - 7 pm
Summer Daily	9 am - 7 pm

Cost

Children under 4	Free
Children Ages 4 - 11	$8.95
Adults	$12.95
Seniors	$11.95
Parking	$3

Discounts for groups of 15 or more.
Call 48 hours in advance.

Plan to spend the day. Take your time. Wear comfortable shoes. Restaurant available, reasonably priced. Or eat at Fuddruckers close by. Be sure to visit the great gift shop with its space memorabilia.

Directions

Located 25 miles south of downtown Houston in Clear Lake, Texas. Take I-45 south. Exit NASA Road One. Go east approximately 3 miles. Will be on the left next to the Johnson Space Center.

TEXAS MEDICAL CENTER TOUR VISITOR INFORMATION AND ASSISTANCE CENTER

1155 Holcombe
713-790-1136

See the world's largest health care center

A tour that will impress. Largest medical health care center in the world. Over 675 acres, all non-profit. Specializes in patient care, education, and research. Employs more than anywhere else in Houston (50,000 jobs). Has a $10 billion impact on our economy. Imagine 10,000 volunteers, 4.5 million patients a year.

Hours

Mon - Thurs	10 am &1 pm
Friday	11 am

By reservation only. Maximum size group is 20.
Tour hours are flexible.

Cost

Free

Watch the video, then tour by van. Tour lasts 1.5 hours. Be sure to ask for directions on where to park and meet. Parking will be validated.

Not recommended for children under ten. Great place to take out-of-town company, like grandparents!

Directions

From 288 South, exit Holcombe and go west to Bertner. Will be on the corner of Holcombe and Bertner. From the 59 Freeway, exit Greenbriar and follow to Holcombe. Go left and continue to Bertner. From the 610 West Loop, exit Bellaire and go east. Bellaire will turn into Holcombe. Follow to Bertner.

TRANSCO TOWER

2800 Post Oak Blvd.
713-850-8841

An observation deck on top of one of Houston's finest skyscrapers

Soars 51 stories high! On a clear day, you'll really see Houston from their observation deck. On top it has a 7,000 watt revolving light that can be seen by all of Houston at night. Below see the famous Water Wall Fountain, it's spectacular, especially after dark. The most photographed scene in Houston.

Hours

Mon - Fri .... 8 am - 6 pm

Cost

Free

Park in the covered parking lot. It's $1 for every hour up to $4.00. Don't worry about which floor to get off; elevators take you directly to the 51st floor. Observation deck faces the west side. Fun. Do it.

Directions

Located directly behind the Galleria or just outside the 610 West Loop (exit Westheimer and go left on S. Post Oak). Will be the highest building in the area.

WORTHAM IMAX THEATER

Hermann Park

713-639-IMAX (4629)

Exciting features on a giant screen!

Six stories high, eighty feet wide, ten times larger than conventional movie screens. Climb Everest. Enter live volcanoes. Explore the Grand Canyon or fly with the Blue Angels. Orbit in space as if you're there. See the new films: Wildfires, Beavers & Migrations. Unique, educational, and entertaining for all. Shows start every hour on the hour.

Hours

Mon - Thurs	10 am - 8 pm
Fri - Sat	10 am - 10 pm
Sunday	11 am - 8 pm

Cost

Children under 11	$4
Adults	$6
Seniors	$4
Members	$3.50
Groups of 20+ (per person)	$3

Get a reservation on weekends! Beware of other activities at the park that might impact parking. Arrive early. Stay and walk through the Museum of Natural Science, go to the Planetarium, see the new Cockrell Butterfly Center, and the Zoo. Gift shops available. Eat at McDonalds inside the museum.

Directions

See directions to Burke Baker Planetarium (page 16).

Locations

1. Anahuac National Wildlife Refuge
2. The Antique Rose Emporium
3. Armand Bayou Nature Center
4. Bayou Wildlife Park
5. Bolivar Ferry
6. Carol's Country Place
7. Edith Moore Nature Sanctuary
8. The Fishing Hole
9. The George Observatory at Brazos Bend
10. Houston Zoological Gardens
11. King's Orchard
12. Matt Family Orchard
13. Mercer Gardens & Arboretum
14. Moorhead's Blueberry Farm
15. Monastery of St. Clare Miniature Horse Farm
16. Nature Discovery Center
17. Nueces Canyon Equestrian Center and Resort
18. Poe's Catfish Farm
19. Robert A. Vines Environmental Science Center
20. Sea Center of Texas
21. Stardust Trail Rides
22. Super Gator Tours
23. Texas Wildlife Rehabilitation Coalition
24. Village Creek Canoe Trips

Chapter 2
GETTING BACK TO NATURE

ANAHUAC NATIONAL WILDLIFE REFUGE

P.O Box 278, Anahuac, Texas
409-267-3337

One of the best places to observe wildlife

Established in 1963 by the U.S. Fish and Wildlife Service. Beautiful. Over 30,000 acres with 12 miles of roads allowing great access for visitors.

One of the best places to see an alligator is in Shoveler Pond. Also see blue herons, white egrets, cattails, roseate spoonbills, nutria, hyacinths. Between October and March, see waterfowl and migratory birds.

Best to view area from your vehicle. No hiking trails. Visitors can walk on the roads. Roads are not suitable for bicycles. Remember the bug repellant. Great fishing. No drinking water available.

The town of Anahuac, a few miles northwest of the refuge is known as the "Alligator Capital of Texas." Each year the town sponsors the Texas Gatorfest. Generally held in September. For more information contact the Chamber of Commerce, 409-267-4190.

Cost

Free

Directions

Located 90 minutes east of downtown Houston, on the northeast shore of East Galveston Bay. From Houston, take Interstate 10 east about 45 miles to Exit 812. Turn south on Texas 61 for four miles, (continue straight) where the road becomes FM 562. Continue south on 562 for eight miles, then east on FM 1985 four miles to the refuge entrance. Watch for sign.

THE ANTIQUE ROSE EMPORIUM

9300 Lueckemeyer Road
Brenham 77833-6453
409-836-5548

An 8-acre scenic garden center

Want great pictures of the kids? The Emporium's one of the best places for that perfect scenic background. It is located on an early settler's homestead. Plan to spend time simply enjoying nature. This retail garden center consists of 8 acres of beautifully landscaped old garden roses, many native plants, old-fashioned cottage perennials, herbs, and a wildflower meadow. Several unique old restored buildings add to the landscaped surroundings. See an 1855 stone kitchen, an 1840s log corncrib, an 1850s salt box house, and a 1900s Victorian home.

Hours

(Closed major holidays)

Mon. - Sat. . . . . 9 am - 6 pm
Sunday . . . . 11 am - 5:30 pm

Cost

Free

Directions

Located on the outskirts of Brenham. Take 290 west of Houston toward Brenham. Exit FM 577 and go north (right) four lights to Highway 105. Take Highway 105 northwest (right) 1.5 miles to FM 50 and go north (left) eight miles. Will be on the right.

ARMAND BAYOU NATURE CENTER

8500 Bay Area Boulevard
281-474-2551

A nature center for children

Surrounded by a large urban area, the Armand Bayou advertises itself as "The Only Wilderness In Town." Educational and entertaining for elementary school children and preschoolers. Spend the morning or afternoon scouting the abundant wildlife that lives here: turtles, fish, snakes, deer, birds, all in their native habitat. Trails include prairie, forest, and marshlands.

Stop at the Interpretive House. Volunteers share interesting facts about the animals. All geared for the younger set. Explore the Martyn Farm, a turn-of-the-century farm on exhibit.

Hours

Monday and Tuesday	Closed
Wed - Sat	9 am - 5 pm
Sunday	Noon to Dusk

Cost

Children under 5	Free
Children ages 5-17	$1
Adults	$2.50
Senior	$1

Admission ends one hour earlier than closing time. Wear comfortable clothes and shoes.

Directions

Located in Clear Lake. Take I-45 South. Exit Bay Area Boulevard. The Nature Center is approximately 6.2 miles east of I-45.

BAYOU WILDLIFE PARK

FM 517, Dickinson, Texas
281-337-6376

You'll love meeting these animals

Ought to be the world's largest petting zoo. Exotic but friendly animals flock to welcome visitors on the open air tram in this 86-acre park. Come meet Ralph the Giraffe, (named after Ralph Sampson, a former Rocket), Tony Llama, Sebastian the Camel, and Suzanne Sommers the White Elk. Not to mention Bonnie, Pancho, Pee Wee, and Shorty. White rhinos that will eat out of your hand. Plus there are ostriches, zebras, water buffalo, rheas, deer, eland, and many more. You will be provided with a running commentary about the animals.

Hours

March 1 through October 30

Daily . . . . 10:00 am - 4:00 pm
Call for Winter Hours & Prices

Cost

March 15 through August 15

Children under 3 . . . . Free
Children ages 3-11 . . . . $5.50
Adults $8.95

Great for elementary age children and preschoolers. Groups welcomed. You will enjoy it. Offers a petting zoo. Come ride the horse. Picnicking area. Wear comfortable clothes and shoes.

Directions

Take Highway 6 South toward Galveston. In Alvin turn left on Highway 35. (Do not take Business 35). Take FM 517 east 3.2 miles. Will be on the right. Or take FM 517 from I-45 and go west 6 miles.

BOLIVAR FERRY

Galveston Island to Bolivar Peninsula (Hwy 87)
409-763-2386

Ride the ferry in Galveston

Fun thing to do with the family or company. Take the Bolivar Ferry from Galveston Island to the Bolivar Peninsula and back. Watch for signs for the Boliver Ferry as you drive on to Galveston Island.

Hours

Seasonal, call ahead.

Cost

Free

Don't wait to drive on if the traffic is heavy. Park in the nearby lot and walk on. From the ferry you will have an excellent view of the harbor. Remember bread for the flock of hungry sea gulls that follow along. Ride takes approximately 20 - 25 minutes one way.

After reaching Bolivar point, drive approximately 1 mile for a view of the old Bolivar Lighthouse. One of only a few left. Built in 1872.

Directions

Located on the east end of Galveston Island. Take I-45 South to Galveston Island. Follow Broadway (as it becomes Seawall Boulevard) past Stewart Beach. Go left on Highway 87/ Ferry Road and watch for signs.

CAROL'S COUNTRY PLACE

1923 Trammel-Fresno Road, Fresno TX
281-431-2664

An adventure in the country

Help with the farm chores like milking the cow, gathering the eggs, feeding the chickens or ducks. Animals are extremely friendly. A must-do for any city kid. Climb the hay loft. Swing on the rope and land in the hay. Slide down the chute. Kids will want to do it again and again. Take the hayride through the woods and pastures to feed the cows and horses. Face painting, pony rides, buggy rides, a petting zoo, and free snow cones. Archery and fishing for the older children. Friendly owner. Take home garden vegetables and eggs. Great place for a birthday party. Tours last 4 hours.

Hours

Call for times and reservations

Cost

(includes all activities)

Child or Adult (Mon - Fri) $5.35
After 3 pm and weekends $6.50

By reservation only. Same age groups are put together. Families can join groups. Wear comfortable old shoes. Casual play clothes. Kids may smell like the animals. Bring sack lunch and cold drinks.

Directions

Located 15 minutes from Astroworld. From the 610 South Loop, exit Almeda Road and go south. Exit Trammel-Fresno Road and go west 2 miles. Will be on the left.

From Highway 6 South, (south of Sugar Land) go left on Hillcroft. Take an immediate right on Trammel-Fresno Road. Go about 2 miles. Will be on the right.

EDITH MOORE NATURE SANCTUARY

440 Wilchester
713-464-4900 (tour information)
713-932-1639 (office)

A nature sanctuary the kids will enjoy

Eighteen acres of nature at its finest. Turtles, raccoons, possums, snakes, frogs, and rabbits. Educational. Considered a teaching sanctuary and part of the Audubon Society. Learn about habitat conservation. Hike the one mile trail. Great for field trips.

Hours

Daily . . . . 8 am - Dusk
Office Hours (weekdays) . . . . 10 am - 4 pm

Cost
Free

Ask for an informative guided tour. Maps can be purchased in the office. Cabin can be rented for birthday parties, weddings, and social occasions.

Directions

Located between Wilcrest and Beltway 8. Exit Memorial Drive from Beltway 8. Go west on Memorial Drive .5 mile. Turn left on Wilchester. Turn left into Sanctuary.

From I-10, exit Wilcrest and go south. Go left on Memorial. Go right on Wilchester. Turn left into Sanctuary.

THE FISHING HOLE

14120 Cypress Rosehill Rd.,
Cypress, Texas 77429
281-373-0123 or 409-836-5471

Go fishing here if you like catfish

Weekly 10,000 to 15,000 lbs. of fish are delivered to fill their two larger than football-field size ponds. This place supplies catfish to all the Fiesta Food Stores in Houston. Great place to take the kids fishing. You can't get catfish any fresher.

Must be serious about catching fish, you buy what you catch. Must bring your own fishing equipment. No rentals. Recommended 14 lb. test line their fish can fight. Remember no glass drinking containers allowed. Wear comfortable shoes.

Hours

Closed Monday and Tuesday

Wed - Sun . . . . 8 am - 6 pm

Cost

No Admission Fee

Fish per pound $2
Cleaned $2.20
Filet $2.40

Bait for sale

Directions

Located in N.W. Houston at the corner of Cypress Rosehill Road and 290. From Beltway 8, exit 290 and turn northwest (away from Houston). Take Cypress Rosehill Road exit. Go to the Cypress Rosehill Road, which is the second stop sign. Turn left (go under the freeway) on Cypress Rosehill.

THE GEORGE OBSERVATORY
BRAZOS BEND STATE PARK

FM 21901, Needville,   409-553-3400

View the stars at Brazos Bend State Park

Life is depriving if you haven't spent a Saturday evening at George Observatory. Part of the Museum of Natural Science. Great activity for the entire family. View the stars through their 36" telescope, one of the largest telescopes in the nation.

Observatory Hours and Costs

Every Saturday

Observatory .... Dusk - 10:00 pm

Tickets for viewing the telescopes go on sale at 5 pm on a first-come-first-served basis. Viewing begins at dark until 10 pm. (Adults $2, Children under 12 $1)

Brazos Bend Park Entrance Fee

Adults $3
Children (under 12) .... free

Pick a Saturday when the sky is clear. Bring your own telescope, lawn chairs, snacks, drinks, and star charts. Star charts are also available for sale. You will also need a flashlight. It is recommended that you cover your flashlight with red cellophane since white light isn't allowed. Also, bring your binoculars. Picnic tables are available. Dress warmly in the winter. Wear comfortable shoes.

Note: The Fort Bend Astronomy Club is generally there with individual members' telescopes set up for public viewing and lectures. Very interesting.

Directions

In Brazos Bend State Park. Take Hwy 59S across the Brazos River to FM 2759 or Crabb River Rd. Exit, go east, and follow the road 20 miles. Ask for map at the Park entrance to find the Observatory.

40

HOUSTON ZOOLOGICAL GARDENS

Hermann Park
513 N. MacGregor, Houston TX 77030
713-284-8300

Houston is proud of her zoo

One of the ten best zoos in the country. Fifty-three acres with a fantastic new gift shop. Visit the Wortham World of Primates, a $7 million exhibit, resembles Africa. The Brown Education Center now offers "Mission Impossible," an exhibit about our vanishing amphibians. Also see the Giraff and the Mexican Wolf exhibits, both are very exciting. Petting zoo, seals, bears, tigers, elephants, giraffes, and tons of other animals.

Plan to spend 3 to 4 hours, maybe the entire day. Wear comfortable shoes. Concession stands inside the zoo offer soft drinks, hamburgers, salads, sandwiches, pizza, frozen yogurt. Cafeteria available. Or bring your own lunch. Plenty of tables for a picnic or bring a blanket and eat in a grassy area. Strollers available at $4 & $7. Wagons $7.

Hours

Daily .... 10 am - 6 pm
Open until 8 pm on Thursday during daylight savings time.

Cost

Free on City Holidays

Children under 2 .... Free
Children ages 2 - 12 .... $.50
Adults $2.50
Seniors $2

Directions

See directions to Burke Baker Planetarium (page 16).

KING'S ORCHARD

Plantersville, Texas
409-894-2766

A wonderful farm where you can pick your own fruit

Two hundred acres just north of Magnolia where you can pick your own strawberries, raspberries, blackberries, peaches, plums, apples, and figs. Picking season begins mid-March.

What's neat about this place is how it was designed with the picker in mind. (Blackberries are grown on special trellis making picking easier.) You'll find this a well run, friendly place.

Providing picnicking areas. Each year more is added to their picking selections. They like suggestions, too.

Great activity for the kids. Be sure to let them know you are coming. Call about 24 hours in advance.

Hours

Tues - Sun .... 8:00 am - 5:00 pm

Directions

Take I-45 North to FM 1488. Exit and travel west 18 miles to Magnolia. Take a right on FM 1774 and travel north for 6 1/2 miles. Turn left at the King's Orchard sign. Go 3/4 mile. The Orchard is located near the Texas Renaissance Festival Grounds.

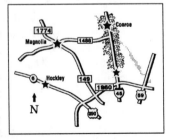

MATT FAMILY ORCHARD

21110 Bauer Hockley Road
Tomball 77375
281-351-7676

Pick-your-own orchard with country fun

Only minutes away from Houston. The Matt Family Orchard offers more than fresh fruits and berries. The farm offers some fun activities for groups. Picnic, roast hot dogs and marshmallows over a campfire, go on a day or night hayride, hike in the woods, or do some birding. See an abundance of wildlife like armadillos, rabbits, coyotes, wild pigs, deer, fox, and bobcats. Reservations are a must. Call at least two weeks in advance.

Other activities, such as a tree swing, a (small) haystack, a tether ball, face painting, and yard games, are popular with children's groups ages 3-8. The farm even offers campouts for teenagers and activities for scouts, family reunions, birthday parties, and playgroups.

Fruits available for picking include figs, thornless blackberries, persimmons, jujube, and in the future chestnuts, Asian pears and mayhaw. The farm plants more every year. The picking season begins in mid-March and runs through November.

Wear comfortable clothes, long pants for the hayride, and athletic shoes. Bring plenty of bug repellent and sunscreen for picking. Ice water is available at the farm.

Hours
Seasonal or any time with a reservation

Cost
Fruit and berries by the pound, groups priced per person

Directions
From Houston, take 290 northwest past 1960 to Mueschke Road. Turn north on Mueschke and go 4.5 miles to Bauer Hockley Road. Go west 1 mile to the orchard.

MERCER GARDENS AND ARBORETUM

22306 Aldine Westfield, Humble, Texas
281-443-8731

Texas' largest and best arboretum

Come see the huge displays of native and cultivated plants and trees. Herb gardens, ferns, flowers. All identified. This is a county park.

Hours

Open daily

Summer	8 am - 7 pm
Sunday	10 am - 7 pm
Winter	8 am - 5 pm

Cost

Free

Beautiful picnic area. Educational. (No pets allowed.)

Directions

Located 1 mile north of 1960 between I-45 North and the 59 Freeway. Take I-45 north and exit 1960. Go east 3 miles to Aldine Westfield. Go left 1 mile. Will be on the right.

MOORHEAD'S BLUEBERRY FARM

19531 Moorhead Road, Conroe, Texas 77302
281-572-1265 or 888-702-0622

A farm where you can pick blueberries

You may want to arrive early in the morning when it is cooler for this adventure. Fifteen acres of blueberries. Established by the late Albert Moorhead. Ask about his blueberry cookbook.

Blueberry picking season generally runs from mid-June through July. Wear comfortable, cool clothes. We recommend wearing a hat. Bring the sun screen. Canteens with ice water will be greatly appreciated. Buckets are provided. Berries are brought home in plastic bags. An hour of picking can produce many pounds of berries. Also available: persimmons, figs, and thornless blackberries.

Hours

Daily . . . . Sunrise to Sunset

Cost

Per Pound (blueberries) $1.25

Directions

Located southeast of Conroe. From Houston, take Highway 59 north. Exit FM 1314 at Porter. Go west about nine miles to Bennette Estates entrance and turn left. Then follow the signs for another three miles.

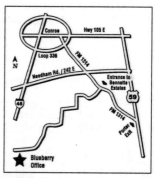

45

MONASTERY OF ST. CLARE MINIATURE HORSE FARM

9300 Highway 105
Brenham 77833
409-836-9652

[handwritten: 1:30-4:00 Tues-Sat]
[handwritten: 979]

Nuns raise miniature horses, sell handmade crafts

[handwritten: Jan Feb Sept First Sat only]

Want a fun Saturday outing? Visit a monastery that raises beautiful miniature horses. While you are there, take the 45-minute tour of the farm. The kids will enjoy petting the miniature horses. The nuns support themselves selling handmade ceramics, too. Be sure to browse through their gift shop. Or sit quietly in the chapel. Bring your lunch, the farm has a picnic area.

Hours

Closed Holy Week and Christmas Day

Daily . . . . 2 pm - 4 pm

Cost

Donations are welcome

Admission . . . . Free

Cost for 45-minute tour

Adults $3
Children under 12 . . . . $1

Directions

Located 9 miles east of Brenham. Take 290 west to Chappell Hill and exit 1155 and go north to 2193. Go west to 105. Will be on 105, on the left.

NATURE DISCOVERY CENTER

7112 Newcastle Bellaire TX 77401
713-667-6550

Delightful for any elementary age children

A four-acre park with herb garden, nature trail, picnic area and playground. Exhibits on vertebrates and invertebrates. See the "touch and guess boxes." Magnet boards, microscopes, and nature books. There is a snake children can handle. Aquariums. Displays of animals bones. Offering so much in the way of activities for kids. Great field trip for schools. Adult programs every first Wednesday of each month from 7:30 until 9:00. Popular for field trip; call before going.

Hours

Monday	Closed
Tues - Fri	Noon - 5:30 pm
Saturday	10:00 am - 5:30 pm
Sunday	Noon - 5:30 pm

Cost

Free

Donations appreciated	$1/person
Field trip or School groups	$2/person

Directions

Located in the City of Bellaire. From the 610 West Loop, take the Evergreen exit and go east. Evergreen Street dead ends at Newcastle. Turn left on Newcastle. Will be shortly on the left.

NUECES CANYON EQUESTRIAN CENTER AND RESORT

9501 U.S. Highway 290 West
Brenham 77833-9138
409-289-2411 • 800-925-5058

A weekend escape only minutes from Houston.

For any out-of-town guest that simply must see Texas. Family friendly — bring the kids. Watch cowboys perform their duties on this 135-acre working ranch, featuring world-class cutting horses competitions. Watch these cowboys and horses in action, in the arena. The ranch offers hayrides, horse riding, and campfire cookouts — barbecue feasts. Or go fishing in the (stocked) lake. Paddleboats. Play volleyball, basketball, and softball. See plenty of longhorn cattle. You'll find the swing under the old oak tree lots of fun.

At the same time, enjoy old-fashion southern hospitality at their bed-and-breakfast inn, with covered porches, and a full-service restaurant. Be sure to order one of their hand-cut-to-your-order steaks. Call for reservations.

Cost

One night's stay $79-100

Directions

Locates 8 miles west of Brenham on Highway 290.

Getting Back To Nature

POE'S CATFISH FARM

FM 359 (Outside Of Hempstead)
409-826-2136

Farm-raised catfish ready for catching

No fishing license required. Bring your fishing pole and bait. Great place to go fishing. Fish from their stock tanks.

Hours

Wed - Sun .... 8 am - 6 pm

Cost

Per pound live weight (fish) $2.15

Must keep all you catch. No minnow or perch bait allowed. Bait sold. Soft drinks.

Directions

Take 290 towards Hempstead. Exit 359. Will be 7 miles south of Hempstead or 2 miles north of Monaville.

ROBERT A. VINES ENVIRONMENTAL SCIENCE CENTER AND ARBORETUM

Spring Branch Independent School District
8856 Westview Drive
Houston 77055
713-365-4175

Small natural science museum with arboretum

See rare and endangered animals from countries like India. See wall murals that explain interesting geological concepts. And a huge collection of fossils, rocks, and minerals from around the world. Exhibits at the center highlight many fascinating environmental subjects. The 4 exhibition halls feature the Oceanography Hall, the Geology Hall, Jack Roach Hall of Exotic Animals, and Wildlife Sciences. If that's not enough to see, explore their 5-acre arboretum, with plants native to the Southern United States and Northern Mexico. Plan to spend an hour.

Hours
(Reservations required)
Mon. - Fri. ....8:30 am - 5 pm

Cost
Free

Directions
Take I-10 east of downtown. Exit Bingle and go right. Turn left on Westview and go 1-1/2 blocks. Will be on the right.

SEA CENTER TEXAS

300 Medical Drive, Lake Jackson, TX 77566
409-292-0100 • 800-792-1112

The world's largest red drum production facility

Opened March 1996, this state-of-the-art facility is the world's largest red drum production facility, capable of producing 20 million fingerlings a year. This $13 million project is a joint adventure of the Dow Chemical Company, Texas Operations, the Texas Parks and Wildlife Department, and the Gulf Coastal Conservation Association.

A popular family and school group destination, with over 4,000 visitors a week. For guided group tours and hatchery tours, call well in advance for reservations. The facility is closed on Mondays.

Features a "touch tank," two 2500-gallon aquariums, two 5000-gallon aquariums, and a 52,000-gallon aquarium. The exhibits explain marine life in Texas' beaches, bays, jetties, and artificial reefs, and out in the Gulf of Mexico. Meet the mascot "Gordon," a 300-pound grouper.

A half-acre youth fishing pond teaches children saltwater fishing. The pond is stocked with drum, seatrout, sheepshead, and croaker. Future exhibits will include an interpretive outdoor wetlands trail.

Hours

Tues.- Fri.	9am - 4pm
Saturday	10am - 5pm
Sunday	1pm - 4pm
Cost	Free

Directions:

At the end of Plantation St., west of Highway 332.

STARDUST TRAILRIDES

3001 Calder Drive, League City TX 77573
281-332-9370

The largest horse rental stable in the Gulf Coast Region

Here you will find a real working ranch offering a great variety of activities for everyone. They feature rides for the beginner and experienced riders, escorted trailrides for groups, hayrides, riding lessons, summer horse camps and more.

On their Taste of Texas Trailride you will see real operating oil wells and longhorn cattle. Midway riders stop for Texas barbecue while sitting around a campfire being serenaded with cowboy songs.

Their Sunset or Moonlight Trailride also features wonderful Texas barbecue and music around a campfire at the end of the day.

The Romantic Adventure includes a horse, a jug of wine and a loaf of bread. Designed for special birthdays, anniversaries, dates, or special occasions.

My favorite is the City Slicker Cattle Drive. Where else could someone go on a two day cattle drive for only $75.00?

Hours to Ride Horses

Sat.- Sun .... 10 am - 6 pm

Trailride Times

10:30 am, noon, 1:30 pm, 3 pm, 4:30 pm, and 6 pm

Cost

Call for prices on trailrides and riding lessons

Horse riding per hour $15.00
Hayrides for 25 people $75.00

This is a great place to take out-of-town guest, who want to experience Texas. Also fun for a family outing, church and office parties.

Directions

Take I-45 toward Galveston. Go two miles past Nasa Road One and exit #22, Calder. Go right on Calder. Stardust Trailrides will be one mile from the freeway.

SUPER GATOR TOURS

108 E. Lutcher Dr., Orange, Texas 77632
409-883-7725

Take a trip by air-boat into the swamp

This thrilling adventure will impress anyone. See huge cypress trees. Also see giant lily pads, turtles, and different kinds of birds. And of course, the trip wouldn't be complete without seeing alligators.

Mr. Floyd, the owner, has over 32 years experience with air boats. In fact, he owns an air boat manufacturing company and enjoys giving tours through the swamp.

Hours
Open daily
Cost

Children under 12 .... $12.88
Adults $23.65

The City of Orange offers some interesting attractions like the Orange Stark Museum of Art at 700 Green Avenue. Featuring Audubon prints of native Texas and Louisiana birds, bronze sculptures by Fredrick Remington, American Indian artifacts, paintings, and more. Be sure to see the First Presbyterian Church. Built by one of the richest women in United States and was the first air conditioned building west of the Mississippi. Fine stained glass windows. A must-see. 800-528-4906

Directions
Located 2 hours east of downtown Houston. Take Interstate 10 east about 115 miles to Orange. Take the last business exit, 878, and make a U-turn under the freeway. Will be on the north side of I-10.

TEXAS WILDLIFE REHABILITATION COALITION

595 Wycliff, Houston, TX 77079
713-468-8622

An organization that helps injured wildlife

Two orphaned baby doves in a neighbor's backyard brought this organization to our attention. The baby birds would have died if it hadn't been for these specially trained experts. Non-profit. Run by local volunteers who nurse many animals to health in their homes. This organization provides a great service to our area wildlife.

Cost

Donations Appreciated

Will give interesting lectures about our local wildlife to any group including children's groups such as scouts and school groups. You will be glad you called them. Ask about Webster the Duck.

Directions

From Beltway 8 (Sam Houston Tollway) exit Memorial Drive and go west. Go apprximately 1.5 miles to Wycliff. Turn right. Will be on your immediate left in the strip mall.

VILLAGE CREEK CANOE TRIPS

FM 418, Kountz, Texas
409-385-6241

A really fun family outing

This may well become an annual event for your family. It has for ours. Invite other families to go with you. Spend the day paddling through the beautiful countryside. Eat lunch on one of many sandy banks. Pull over to swing from a rope into the water. This canoe trip is fun.

Costs

Canoe or Kayak $20
(includes canoe or kayak, paddles, life vests, and a shuttle ride)

Hours

Seasonal, call for reservations.

Note: a canoe holds approximately 2 adults, 1 cooler, and 2 small children. Great for everyone but the very small. Gentle current. Paddle time is about 3 to 4 hours but allow 6 for lunch and letting the kids swim. We like to be underway by 10:00 am.

We suggest that you duct-tape your cooler lid before you leave so the lid won't come off. There is a Dairy Queen in Kountz. Good place to stop before heading home. Longer and other canoe trips are available.

Directions

Note: The input and takeout points vary. Be sure to call for directions.

Take I-10 going east from Houston. *Take Highway 61 north to Highway 90 going east, to Highway 326, which will take you to Kountz. You will come to a traffic light that junctions 69 and 326. Go left (north) on 69 and continue until almost out of town. Turn right on FM 418 and go .25 mile. Village Creek Canoe Rental will be on the right. Watch for sign.*

Locations

1. Allen's Landing Park
2. Bayou Bend Collection
3. Byzantine Fresco Chapel Museum
4. Contemporary Arts Museum
5. The Children's Museum of Houston
6. Forbidden Gardens
7. Fort Bend Museum
8. George Bush Presidential Library and Museum
9. George Ranch Historical Park
10. Heritage Museum of Montgomery County
11. Historic Morton Cemetery
12. Holocaust Museum Houston
13. Houston Fire Museum
14. The Menil Collection
15. Military Museum of Texas
16. The Museum of Fine Arts, Houston
17. Museum of Health & Medical Science
18. The Museum of Printing History
19. The Museum of Southern History
20. Rice University Art Gallery
21. Rothko Chapel
22. Washington-on-the-Brazos Historical Park

Chapter 3
MUSEUMS AND HISTORY

ALLEN'S LANDING PARK

1001 Commerce

Historical site marking Houston's beginning

Dedicated to the place where Houston began, in 1836. Behind the Old Spaghetti Warehouse Restaurant at the foot of Main Street, see where the Allen Brothers bought land. Capitalizing on the popularity of Sam Houston, they named their settlement-to-be after this great hero.

24 Hour Access

Cost
Free

Located on the banks of the Buffalo Bayou. Allen's Landing is not in the best part of downtown. This is best seen from your car.

Call **Whitewater Experience**, 713-774-1028, located at 6005 Cypress St., Houston, TX 77074 for information on canoe rentals and launch sites. From a canoe, see one of the best views of downtown from the bayou. Also they offer information on other exciting places to go canoeing in our area.

Directions
Located downtown at Milan and Commerce.

BAYOU BEND COLLECTION

1 Westcott
713-639-7750

Houston's prize American arts collection

Part of the Museum of Fine Arts. You are invited to see this collection in its permanent setting at the renovated house of Ima Hogg. See prized, rare objects and art, making this collection one of the three most respected among art historians.

Hours

Call for times and to make reservations

No children under 10 are admitted in the Museum except on "Open House" days and on "Family Days." On these days special activities will be provided for them.

Cost

Family Days (every third Sun) ...... Free
Children ages 10 - 18 .... $5
Adults $10
Seniors $8.50

Directions

From the 610 West Loop, exit Memorial Drive. Go east. Turn south at Westcott and proceed to the parking lot. Cross the footbridge to the grounds.

BYZANTINE FRESCO CHAPEL MUSEUM

4011 Yupon
713-521-3990

See 13th Century frescos in Houston

What's unique about these frescos? No other frescos from this period— this size and quality—exists in the Western Hemisphere. This $4 million building houses two unique frescos from the 13th Century. Once hanging in the Church of Cyprus, the two fresco, now claim Houston as their home. Open to the public.

Hours

Wed. - Sun. . . . . 11 am - 6 pm

Cost

Free
(Donations appreciated)

Directions

Located at the corner of Branard and Yupon Streets, 4 blocks west of Montrose and 2 blocks south of West Alabama.

CONTEMPORARY ARTS MUSEUM

5216 Montrose
713-284-8250

Come see contemporary art at its finest

Located next door to the Museum of Fine Arts, in the Museum District. A variety of photography, paintings, sculpture, and lectures. Visit the gift shop. Come see, recently renovated.

Hours
Closed on Monday

Tues, Wed, Fri, & Sat	10 am - 5 pm
Thursday	10 am - 9 pm
Sunday	Noon - 5 pm

Cost
Free

Directions

Located in the Museum District next to the Museum of Fine Arts. From the 59 Freeway exit S. Shepherd/Greenbriar. Take Greenbriar south to the 1st light (Bissonnet) and turn left. Follow about 1.5 miles to Montrose Blvd. Will be on the corner.

THE CHILDREN'S MUSEUM OF HOUSTON

1500 Binz
713-522-1138

A museum for children

We should have had a place like this when we were kids. Located in the Museum District in its fantastic facility. Fascinating hands-on exhibits like a grocery store with shopping carts and cash register. Experience living in a different country or on a farm. Plan to spend time. Very educational. Bring the video camera.

Hours

Closed Monday (except federal holidays)

Tues - Sat . . . . 9 am - 5 pm
Thurs *(Free Family Night)* . . . . 5 pm - 8 pm
Sunday . . . . Noon - 5 pm

Cost

Children under 2 . . . . Free
Children 2 and older $5
Seniors $4
Members . . . . Free
Discount rate after 3 pm daily $3
Thursday 5 pm - 8 pm . . . . Free

Parking is $3 ($1 for members) with a valid museum ticket.

Ask about their special programs and classes. One of the best places to have a birthday party (for members only).

Directions

From the 59 Freeway northbound, exit Fannin and go south to Binz. Turn left. Will be 4 blocks down.

From 288 southbound, exit Calumet and go right on Binz. Will be 3 blocks on the left.

FORBIDDEN GARDENS

23500 Franz Road, Katy TX
281-347-8000

An outdoor museum with replicas of the Forbidden City and Emperor Qin's Tomb

In 1973, a farmer in China accidentally uncovers one of the most exciting archaeological findings of our century. He discovered seven thousand magnificent life-size terra cotta soldiers and horses, battle ready, standing guard over Emperor Qin's Tomb.

Right here in Houston, see an unbelievable recreation of the emperor's tomb and these remarkable soldiers. Crazy or not about archaeology, Forbidden Gardens will provide you with a rare adventure into the heart of ancient China.

Also see an authentic model of the Forbidden City, done in great detail. A 30-minute video explains all you would want to know and more about these fantastic dwellings. I highly recommend taking their tour. Tours starts every hour on the hour. Watch for additional exhibits as the museum plans to expand.

Hours
Wed - Sun .... 10 am - 4 pm

Cost
Adults .... $ 10
Seniors 60+ .... $ 5
Children ages 6-18 .... $ 5
Group rates for 25 or more .... $ 5

Wear comfortable shoes. A jug of ice water comes in handy, especially in the summer. You will enjoy this one-of-a-kind museum experience.

Directions
Take I-10 west to the Grand Parkway exit. Go north to Franz Road and go left. Will be immediately on the right.

FORT BEND MUSEUM

500 Houston Street, Richmond TX
281-342-6478

A great museum on local history

Just as prestigious as its history. The Fort Bend Museum is one of the highest certified museums in our country. Find yourself back in the days of Stephen F. Austin as he builds Fort Bend on the Brazos River. Great displays. Interesting. Educational. You leave feeling you're a history buff. Note the artifacts from Civil War days.

Visiting the Fort Bend Museum should include the Moore House. Built on a sugar cane plantation in 1905, in the Victorian style of the time. Renovated in the 1920's to the then more popular Neoclassic style. Amid huge, beautiful oaks. Presently, the house is under renovation - call ahead. You will enjoy every moment.

Hours

Tues - Fri	9 am - 5 pm
Saturday	10 am - 5 pm
Sunday	1 pm - 5 pm

Cost

Museum and guided tour of Moore House, Smith Cottage

Children under 3	Free
Children ages 3 - 12	$2
Adult	$3
Seniors	$2.50

Small, plan to spend forty-five minutes to an hour to see it all.
Noted as one of the best small museums in Texas.

Directions

Located 35 minutes from downtown Houston. Go west on 90 A across the Brazos River into Richmond. You will see the courthouse. Turn left past the courthouse and go two blocks to Houston Street. You will be able to see the Museum.

GEORGE BUSH PRESIDENTIAL LIBRARY AND MUSEUM

1000 George Bush Dr. W., College Station TX 77845
409-260-9552 • www.csdl.tamu.edu/bushlib

A presidential library near Houston

Texas—the only state that's home to two of the ten presidential libraries in the United States. Visit the George Bush Presidential Library and Museum, part of the Texas A&M campus in College Station. This beautiful 17,000-square-foot facility houses many items and documents pertaining to President Bush's distinguished public career. He served as a congressman, an Ambassador to the United Nations, as the Chief of the U.S. Liaison Office in China, as Chairman of the Republican National Committee, as Director of the Central Intelligent Agency, as Vice-President and as President of the United States.

Watch home movies of President Bush's youth. See many interesting displays and memorabilia from the Persian Gulf War-Desert Storm, Air Force One, his office, and much more. One section, dedicated to our popular First Lady, Barbara Bush, displays her inaugural gowns and tells of her efforts in literacy.

The library, less then two hours from Houston, makes a great family outing. Plan to spend a couple hours at the museum. While in College Station, eat at Freebirds on University Street — a favorite eatery with giant burritos made the way you like them.

Hours

Closed Thanksgiving Day, Christmas Day, New Year Day

Mon. - Sat. .... 9:30 am - 5 pm
Sunday .... Noon - 5pm

Cost

Adults $3
Students 17+ $2.50
Seniors 62+ $2.50
Groups $2.50
Children under 16 & School Groups Free

Directions

Take 290 NW to Hwy 6 (Hempstead) and go north to Bryan College Station. Go left on George Bush Dr (past Wellborn). Will be on the right.

GEORGE RANCH HISTORICAL PARK

10215 FM 762, Richmond, Texas
281-343-0218

The Texian Market Days event is fantastic

Ever been to a living museum? Five hundred acres of wonderfulness. Get a taste of ranch life back in the 1820's to 1940's. Open April through December for public tours. Out in the beautiful countryside. Well worth the drive. See the Victorian mansion. The country store. The animals. Wear your western duds. Grab the camera. Something for the entire family. You'll enjoy the horse-drawn wagons that take you through a tour of how life use to be.

Be sure to mark your calendar and come to their annual celebrations and events. These are the best times to visit the ranch. Especially their Texian Market Days held in October. Streets filled with crafts and food. Watch blacksmiths at work. Calf roping. Tour the homes. An event you won't want to miss. Here are some of their events:

April	Traditional Victorian Easter Egg Hunt
July 4	Independence Day
October	Texian Market Days
December	Campfire Christmas

Hours

Sat and Sun .... 10 am

Cost

Children under 3	Free
Children ages 3-12	$3
Adults	$6
Seniors	$5

Directions

Located one hour southwest of downtown Houston. Take Highway 59 South across the Brazos River to Crabb River Road, Fm 2759. Exit, go east, and follow the road approximately 20 miles.

HERITAGE MUSEUM OF MONTGOMERY COUNTY

1506 I-45 North, Conroe 77301
409-539-6873

Let your kids be a pioneer for the day

Ever hear of Dr. Charles Stewart? As a resident of Montgomery County, he designed our Lone Star Flag and the Texas Seal. See his drawings at this fantastic little museum. It offers any visitor an interesting look into the frontier days of the 3rd county in Texas.

Once a part of Mexico, Montgomery County played an important part in the history of Texas. As the site for Stephen F. Austin's last colony, the county consisted of settlers eager to grow cotton. Huge sawmills developed. And most of all, oil was discovered. Conroe was once the 3rd largest oil field in our country. Now, Lake Conroe and the Woodlands add to their list of developments.

The museum features three galleries, with a permanent exhibit and a hands-on general store and log cabin for children. Kids pretend to keep the store, cook on a hearth, dress-up, and more. Sign-up for Pioneer Days the Monday after the 4th of July. The list of popular activities includes candlemaking, quilting, marble games, washing on a wash board.

Hours

(Closed holidays)

Mon. and Tues. . . . . Reservations only
Wed - Sat. . . . . 9 am - 4 pm

Cost

Adults $1
Children under 12 . . . . $.50

Directions

Located north of the intersection of I-45 and 105 on the feeder. From Houston, take I-45 north and exit #87. Stay on the feeder.

HISTORIC MORTON CEMETERY
RICHMOND HISTORIC DISTRICT
Second Street, Richmond
281-342-6478
Famous Texas pioneers buried here

Indulge in some interesting Texas history. Only minutes from downtown visit the old gravesite of Jane Long, the Mother of Texas. See the final resting-place for many well-known early Texas settlers. The Morton Cemetery's list of who's who' will impress anyone Here lies Mirabeau B. Lamar, William Kinchen Davis, Thomas Jefferson Smith, the Moore Family, Walter M. Burton, Mamie and Albert George, Robert Gillespie, and Clem Bassett.

Stop at the Fort Bend County Museum, 500 Houston Street, in Richmond, for a map and brochure of the cemetery. Plan to do some gravestone rubbings; the museum supplies the materials. This was lots of fun.

Ask about a tour of the cemetery, the courthouse, the Moore Home, and the Long Cottage. Tour can be arranged through the museum.

Hours
Daily .... 10 am - 5 pm

Cost for tour
Adults $3
Children under 12 .... $2
Children under 3 .... Free

Directions
Located in Richmond. Take Highway 90-A west of Houston, across the Brazos River to Second Street. Go north.

HOLOCAUST MUSEUM HOUSTON

5401 Caroline
713-942-8000

A museum designed to educate about the Holocaust

Opening March 1996, the third of its kind in our country, (one in Washington D.C., New York City, and in the future, Los Angeles) Cost $7 million.

Over 350 Houstonians survived Nazi concentration camps. The museum tells some of their stories on a 35-minute video presentation. Offering permanent and visiting art and displays, along with a lending library and sculpture garden. The facility is designed to appear as a Nazi death camp. Note the smokestack-like structure of a crematorium as you approach the museum. I recommend this activity for children over ten years of age. Be prepared to answer their questions.

Hours

Mon - Fri . . . . 9 am - 5 pm
Sat & Sun . . . . Noon - 5 pm

Cost
Free

The object of the Museum is to educate our generation and upcoming generations about what happened to the Jews. Well-presented.

Directions
Located in the Museum District, directly behind the Museum of Natural Science. From the 59 Freeway northbound, exit Greenbriar and go south. Go left on Bissonnet and follow to Caroline. (Bissonnet becomes Binz.) Go left, will be one block down.

HOUSTON FIRE MUSEUM

2403 Milam Street
713-524-2526

See what fire fighting was like in the old days

One hundred fifty years of fire-fighting artifacts. See old fire trucks. Located in a former fire station south of downtown Houston.

Staffed by friendly firefighters. Tours provided for groups of ten or more with reservations. Be sure to take the kids and grandparents.

Small gift shop. Check out their t-shirts and hats. Ask about having a birthday party there.

Hours

Tuesday - Saturday . . . . 10 am - 4 pm
Closed most holidays, Sundays, and Mondays

Cost

Children ages 3-17 . . . . $1
Adults $2

Directions

Located south of downtown between West Gray and McGowen.

THE MENIL COLLECTION

1511 Branard
713-525-9400

A fantastic art museum

Ask who has seen the Menil Collection? Chances are nobody you know has ever heard of it. One of our great fine art museums. It features art from the Antiquities, the Byzantine Period, Tribal Cultures, Surrealism, and even some paintings by Picasso. Beautifully housed; nicely displayed.

Hours

Wed - Sun . . . . 11 am - 7 pm

Cost

Free

Take the kids. No brochures or recordings to guide you. Friendly guides eagerly share their knowledge.

Offers guest exhibits, particularly from surrounding universities. Don't forget to see the Rothko Chapel next door and the Book Store across the street on Branard.

Directions

Located between Shepherd and Montrose in the 1500 block of West Alabama. From the 59 Freeway, exit South Shepherd and go north. Turn right on West Alabama. Turn right on Mandell. Go one block, turn left. (Be careful where you park, you can be ticketed).

MILITARY MUSEUM OF TEXAS

6040 Brittmoore Suite B
Houston 77041
713-466-0901

Visit this small, but growing museum

Ever see a Huey Helicopter up close? This museum prides itself in the preservation of military memorabilia, particularly military vehicles. The museum collects and restores military vehicles-most are operable, too. See many of these restored vehicles as they participate in parades, school projects, veteran's events, and other special occasions throughout the area.

The museum collects military items from all our country's military conflicts. Small (in a temporary location), it is located in two buildings: one for display, one for restoring. If you're interested in our military history, you'll find this museum interesting. Best of all, visitors are welcome to climb aboard — it's all hands on. Call before going.

Hours

(Open Saturdays upon request)
Mon. - Fri. . . . . 9 am - 5pm

Cost

Adults $2
Children under 12 . . . . $1

Directions

Take the Sam Houston Tollway to the Clay Road exit. Go 1 block west to Brittmoore. Go north 1 mile. Will be on the right in the Brittmoore Business Park Complex.

THE MUSEUM OF FINE ARTS, HOUSTON

1001 Bissonnet
713-639-7300

A great fine arts museum

One place in Houston you will want to return to again and often. A wealth of art. Spills into other parts of Houston. One of our country's finest. Their visiting exhibitions, such as "Art at Work: 40 Years of the Chase Manhattan Collection" will keep you coming. Ask for their advance exhibition schedule. Thursdays are free.

Hours

Closed Monday

Tues, Wed, & Fri, Sat . . . . 10 am - 5 pm
Thursday . . . . 10 am - 9 pm
Sunday . . . . 12:15 pm - 6 pm

Cost

Children under 6 . . . . Free
Children ages 6 - 18 . . . . $1.50
Adults $3
Members . . . . Free

All kinds of tours offered. Docent tours, call for times. Interest your children in art with the "Post Card Tour," a fun game. Museum also includes the **Bayou Bend Collection, The Glassell School of Art, Lillie and Hugh Roy Cullen Sculpture Garden.**

Directions

Located at the corner of Bissonnet and Montrose. From the 59 Freeway, exit South Shepherd/Greenbriar. Take Greenbriar south to the 1st light (Bissonnet) and turn left and go about 1 1/2 miles. Cross Montrose. Get in the left lane and turn left into parking lot. Museum will be across the street.

MUSEUM OF HEALTH AND MEDICAL SCIENCE

1515 Hermann Drive   713-521-1515

An exciting museum about the amazing human body

Open March 1996, this museum is sponsored by the Harris County Medical Society, an organization for physicians in our area. Offering the Amazing Body Pavilion where you tour through the human body. Plenty of hands-on exhibits like the 10-foot-tall walk through brain or the Clogged Artery Station. You will be in a 22-foot rib cage. There are 30 interactive audio and video kiosks, also huge sculptures of human organs. Great activity for families, especially children age 8 or over.

Hours

Closed Mon, Thanksgiving, & Christmas

Tues - Sat . . . . 9 am - 5 pm
Thurs . . . . 9 am - 7 pm
Sun . . . . Noon - 5 pm

Tour Costs

FREE Admission: Thurs 4 pm - 7 pm
Group rates available

Children ages 4-12 (under 4 free) $3
Students and Seniors $3
Adults (12 and older) $4
Members . . . . FREE

Be sure to see the feature playing in the McGovern Theater. Excellent films. See the Amazing Body Gift Shop. Select a healthy snack from the Health Hut.

Directions

Southbound on Hwy 59, exit Greenbriar and go south. Turn left on Bissonnet (becomes Binz.) Stay on Binz until you come to La Branch, go right.

Northbound, take the Richmond/Fannin exit and go south on Fannin. Turn left on Binz and then right on La Branch.

THE MUSEUM OF PRINTING HISTORY

1324 West Clay Street, Houston 77019
713-522-4652

Visit one of our most unique museums

Learn how to bind a book or work an early printing press. Or how paper came to be and what books looked like in the 1600s. The collection includes many rare items like pages from a Gutenberg Bible and the first printed children's book. The museum takes you from early papyrus paper and the Rosette Stone of the ancient world through the industrial ages to our modern age. Understand how the printed word's effect on history is anything but dull. A must-see. Drop-ins are welcome. The museum is popular with school groups.

The museum offers guest the opportunity to see fine art facsimiles of **The Book of Kells, Marco Polo's Book of Wonder** and **The Gutenberg Bible**. Be sure to see the 45-minute video—a well-done presentation that will fascinate you and the kids. Plan to take your time.

Caution. The museum's small parking lot fills up easily; beware of the no parking signs on the streets.

Hours

Closed Monday

Tues - Sun. . . . . 10 am - 5 pm

Cost

Adults $2
Children under 12 . . . . $1
Seniors $1

Directions

From Memorial Drive, go south on Waugh to W. Clay Street. Go left. Will be on the left.

THE MUSEUM OF SOUTHERN HISTORY

14070 SW Frwy, Sugar Land TX 77478
281-269-7171

Sugar Land's new museum

All ages find this museum exciting. Learn about the South as you take the 1 ½ hour tour. See artifacts from the 1860s, many from the Civil War. Items at the museum include an extensive collection of handguns, quilts (one made from a Confederate Soldier's uniform), medical equipment and supplies, money, and much more.

The museum includes a permanent collection, the Stephen F. Austin Community Room, and a room for traveling exhibits. Exhibits on loan come from interesting private collections or other museums in the country. See an authentic sharecropper's cabin. It originated from a farm in the area, and houses many unique tools from early frontier days. Sharecropping in Fort Bend County existed until the 1950s.

Call ahead for the guided tour. Drop-ins are welcome. The museum is popular with school groups as well as senior citizens. Take the family.

Hours

Tues - Thurs	10 am - 4 pm
Sat - Sun	1 pm - 4 pm

Cost

Children under 5	Free
Children ages 6-12	$2
Adults	$3
Seniors	$2

Directions

Southbound on Hwy 59, exit Sugar Creek /90A. Take the feeder street through the light (Dairy Ashford) and watch for the Southern National Bank on your right. Turn into the bank. Museum is behind the bank in a separate building.

RICE UNIVERSITY ART GALLERY

Sewall Hall, Rice University
6100 Main Street
713-527-6069

Gain an appreciation for contemporary art

Outstanding contemporary works exhibit at the Rice University Art Gallery. Not always, but many times exhibit themes will interest families. Some gear to children. Be sure to visit the Gallery on those occasions. Art exhibits in a large room. Visiting artist often paint a specific piece for the exhibit on site. Tour on your own, or call ahead and ask for a tour. The staff will eagerly answer any questions, too.

Hours

Mon. - Fri.(Thurs 'til 8pm)	11 am - 5 pm
Saturday	11 am - 5 pm
Sunday	Noon - 5 pm

Cost

Free

Directions

Located on the Rice University campus. On Main Street, between Rice and University Boulevards, take Entrance #1. You'll see the Lovett Hall Administration Building, with the arches. Sewall Hall locates next door. Park in any visitor parking space.

ROTHKO CHAPEL

3900 Yupon Street
713-524-9839

Visit this unique chapel

While visiting the Menil Art Collection see the Rothko Chapel next door. A work of art in itself. Original. Inside featuring fourteen abstract paintings by Mark Rothko. Note the subdued lighting and structural shape creating a meditative atmosphere. Almost cave-like. Sit for a while or simply view the paintings.

Don't forget to see the Broken Obelisk, Barnett Newman's steel sculpture outside. Dedicated to Martin Luther King.

Hours

Open daily including holidays
10 am - 6 pm

Cost

Free

Directions

Located next to the Menil Museum. Between Shepherd and Montrose in the 1400 block of West Alabama. From the 59 Freeway, exit S. Shepherd and go north. Turn right on West Alabama. Turn right on Yupon. Go one block.

WASHINGTON-ON-THE BRAZOS HISTORICAL PARK STAR OF THE REPUBLIC MUSEUM

FM 1155, Washington TX 77880
409-878-2461 • 409-878-2214

Historical park and museum in Washington County

Visit the birthplace of Texas. See where the signing of the Texas Declaration of Independence took place on March 2, 1836, declaring our independence from Mexico. For the next ten years (1836-1846) the Republic of Texas proudly existed as a nation.

The Historical Park features the visitor complex, the Independence Hall, and the Star of the Republic Museum. With plenty of hands-on displays, audio-visual presentations, and interactive exhibits, the museum offers visitors a better understanding of the Texas Republic and Texas history. Special tours and programs can be arranged.

Admission to the park is free and opens daily from 8 am to dusk year-around. Bring a lunch, the park offers a delightful picnic ground under huge old oak trees.

Join the Texas Independence Day celebration in March. Enjoy live music, food, and crafts. Call for date and details.

Museum Hours

(Closed Thanksgiving and Christmas through the New Year's Day)
Daily . . . . 10 am - 5 pm

Museum Cost

Adults $4
Students $2
Children under 6 . . . . Free

Directions

Take 290 west to Highway 6. Go north to Highway 105 (Navasota.) Take 105 west towards Brenham — 7 miles to FM 1155. Go south 2 miles. Will be on the left.

Exit FM 577 and go north (right) 4 light to Highway 105. Take Highway 105 northwest (right) 1 1/2 miles to FM 50 and go north (left) 8 miles. Will be on the right.

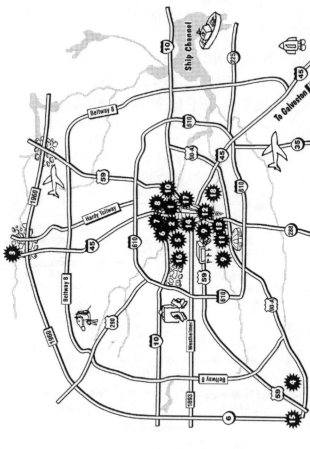

Location

1. Aerial Theatre at Bayou Place
2. The Alley Theatre
3. Cynthia Woods Mitchell Pavilion
4. Fort Bend Community Theater
5. Gilbert & Sullivan Society of Houston
6. Houston Ballet
7. Houston Grand Opera
8. Houston Symphony Orchestra
9. Main Street Theater
10. MasterCard Broadway Series
11. Miller Outdoor Theater
12. Radio Music Theater
13. Rice University Players
14. River Performing and Visual Arts Center
15. Shakespeare by the Book Festival
16. Stages Repertory Theater
17. Theatre Under the Stars
18. University of Houston's Wortham Theater

AERIAL THEATRE AT BAYOU PLACE

520 Texas Avenue
713-230-1600

Modern theater with live entertainment

Aerial Theatre is one of Houston's newest places for live entertainment. With a versatile floor plan, the theatre offers a wide variety of seating arrangements to fit its entertainment at hand. Appealing to all audiences; many shows are family oriented. See musicals, comedies, concerts, films, and theatrical productions. The theatre is part of a 130,000 square-foot complex — Bayou Place —that includes 3 restaurants, a café, and a movie theater. Call for a schedule of upcoming events from time to time.

Directions

Located in the heart of the Theater District, downtown, between Bagby and Smith Streets.

THE ALLEY THEATRE

615 Texas Avenue, 77002
713-228-9341 (Info)
713-228-8421 (Tickets)

Houston's largest and oldest professional theater

This theater began in an alley and has since become one of the top ten professional theaters in our nation. And for a good reason. Many a Broadway hit began here, like ***Dr. Jekyll and Mr. Hyde.*** This is Houston's only resident professional repertory theater company. Offering two stages and a large variety of works.

Buy season tickets and enjoy some of the finest in plays. Other benefits like coupons for dining make going a treat.

Watch the newspapers for unbelievable discounts such as "pay what you want" days. Sometimes you can get 1/2 price tickets the day of the performances. Weekdays are less. Call for more information and details.

Shows start promptly. Those coming late are seated in the back.

Directions

Located downtown on Texas Avenue and Lousiana Avenue in the Theater District.

CYNTHIA WOODS MITCHELL PAVILION

2005 Lake Robins
713-629-3700 (Ticket Master)
or 281-363-3300

Outdoor amphitheater offering great entertainment

Opened in 1990. An outdoor amphitheater with seating for 13,000 (with 3,000 covered seats).

Offering symphony and ballet, country western music, to some of the biggest names in rock groups.

Their annual Children's Festival is always a huge success. Featuring puppets, music and dancing. Watch for their laser shows. Always something happening.

Times and prices of performances vary. Call for information. Tickets can be purchased at any Foleys, Fiesta, Kroger, or Ticket Master as well as at their box office.

Directions

Located in the Woodlands. From Houston take the Hardy Toll Road or I-45 North going north. Exit the Woodlands Parkway. Continue north on the feeder. You will come to an underpass, go under and immediately turn right. The road will circle around and you will be going west. You are now on the Woodlands Parkway. Go to the 3rd stop light. Someone will be there to direct traffic.

FORT BEND COMMUNITY THEATER

2815 N. Main Avenue (Hwy 90A)
Stafford TX
281-208-3333

Offering family entertainment

Adding your name to their mailing list will give you a lot to look forward to. Enthusiastic, non-profit, fast growing community theater. All amateurs. Children's matinees performing childhood favorites. Reserve yourself a seat for the *The Crucible* and enjoy the Halloween season. Christmas plays.

Acting lessons offered to all. In a great location. Nice. Discount rates for groups.

Cost

Children's plays $5
Per Person $5

For weekend evening performances offering family entertainment

Children ages 5 - 12 .... $5
Seniors $7
Adults $8

Directions

Located in Stafford in a historical building. From the Southwest Freeway, exit Hwy 90A and go south past 1092. Turn left on Avenue G. Turn left again on 90A. Will be shortly on the left. Park in front.

Houston Has *Talent*

GILBERT AND SULLIVAN SOCIETY OF HOUSTON

4265 San Felipe
713-627-3570

Enjoy W. S. Gilbert's wit and Arthur Sullivan's music

The Society's humble beginning included a handful of volunteers and a gymnasium without air conditioning. The Society now claims internationally recognition as an amateur opera company. See their performances (***The Pirates of Penzance, The Mikado, HMS Pinafore, Princess Ida, Iolanthe***) in the Wortham Center.

English actor, Alister Donkin, spends his summers in Houston. He serves as both the stage director and featured performer.

Watch for their annual performances (6 in all) held in July. Purchase tickets early, they sell out quickly. Call for ticket information. The box office opens in July. 713-238-2323

Cost

Tickets . . . . $12 - $30

Directions

Performed at the Wortham Center, 510 Preston, located downtown in the Theater District at the intersection of Texas and Smith Streets.

Houston Has ♫ *Talent*

HOUSTON BALLET

Wortham Theater
510 Preston, Houston 77002
713-523-6300

Houston has a wonderful ballet company

The Houston Ballet offers fabulous productions in the Wortham Center. It has become the nation's fourth largest dance company, performing in New York, Europe, and even in China. Their ballet academy is located at 1916 West Gray. Classes offered for children/adults. Season runs August through June.

Ticket Information

For schedule and tickets call 713-227-ARTS. Tickets bought 5 days in advance will be mailed to you, otherwise tickets are pick-up at the box office the night of the show.

Directions

The Wortham Theater is located at the intersection of Texas Avenue and Smith Street, in the Theater District

HOUSTON GRAND OPERA

Wortham Theater
510 Preston, Houston 77002
713-546-0246

Houston has a great opera

The Houston Grand Opera is a world-renowned opera company. Classical as well as modern works, even contemporary works by Houstonians. Season runs from early October into May. Christmas time is especially great. Ticket prices range from $26 to $176.

Performances are in the beautiful Wortham Center. Operas at this ultra-modern facility provide English subtitles (like in movies) above the stage area, since works are often performed in their original language.

There generally is a walk-up buffet in the lobby that opens an hour and a half before the performance begins.

Ticket Information

For schedule and tickets call 713-227-Arts. Tickets bought 5 days in advance will be mailed to you, otherwise tickets are pick-up at the box office the night of the show.

Directions

The Wortham Theater is located at the intersection of Texas Avenue and Smith Street, in the Theater District.

Houston Has Talent

HOUSTON SYMPHONY ORCHESTRA

Jones Hall
615 Louisiana, Houston 77002
713-224-4240

One of the best symphonies

Miss Ima Hogg founded the Houston Symphony in 1913. Since then it has become a world-class symphony. The Houston Symphony performs in the newly renovated Jones Hall, offering its classical repertoire from September to May and its Pop Series of lighter favorites from May through July.

Some rehearsals are open to the public for a nominal fee. Free performances at the Miller Outdoor Theater are offered during the summer.

Ticket Information

For schedule and tickets call 713-227-ARTS Tickets bought 5 days in advance will be mailed to you, otherwise tickets are pick-up at the box office the night of the show.

Directions

Jones Hall is located downtown in the Theater District at the intersection of Capitol Ave. & Louisiana St.

Houston Has Talent

MAIN STREET THEATER
2540 Times Blvd. & 4617 Montrose
713-524-6706

Houston's best intimate theater

Great plays for both adults and children. Has the long-est running children's series in Houston. Classic and contemporary works. Also offering a touring production that visits schools throughout the year.

Season runs from September through May with some summer shows. Local professional actors used.

Discounts are available for groups of 10 or more.

Hours - Call for shows and show times.

Cost

Children's shows

Adult $8
Children to age 18 . . . . $6

Adult shows

Wednesday Preview $6.50
Thursday $13
Friday and Saturday $18
Sunday $14

Directions

Directions to the Montrose location in Chelsea Market:

Southbound on Hwy 59: *Exit Fanin and go south. Turn right (west) on Binz (becomes Bissonnet) and then turn right (north) on Montrose. The theater is behind the Redwood Grill Restaurant, before Hwy 59.*

Northbound on Hwy 59: *From the Downtown Louisiana Spur exit Richmond. Turn left (west) on Richmond then left (south) on Montrose. The theater will be on the left before Bissonnet.*

Directions to Times location in the Rice Village:

From the 59 Freeway, exit Kirby and go south. Go one block past Rice Boulevard to Times Boulevard and go left. Will be on the left.

Houston Has ♪ Talent

MASTERCARD BROADWAY SERIES

Jones Hall, 615 Louisiana
Season tickets 713-622-SHOW (7469)
Ticketmaster 713-629-3700

Broadway shows in Houston

Houston loves Broadway shows. We're high on the list of stops for touring Broadway productions. Thanks to the MasterCard Broadway Series, Broadway hits—many blockbusters—come to Houston. Most tickets are purchased as season tickets for approximately six productions a year. Individual tickets are sold after that through Ticketmaster.

Season tickets go on sale April.

Cost

Season package $194-338
Individual ticket range . . . . $40 - 70

Directions

Jones Hall is located downtown in the Theater District at the intersection of Capitol Avenue and Louisiana Street.

Houston Has **♪** *Talent*

MILLER OUTDOOR THEATRE

Hermann Park
100 Concert Dr. 77030-1702
P.O. Box 66267 77266
713-284-8351 (Summer Schedule)
713-284-8350 (Program Line)

An outdoor theater offering free entertainment

Be sure to plan this into your summer. The price is right. Free. Call and get a summer schedule. Here is a sample of what they may be offering:

In June and July the Houston Symphony Orchestra puts on perforamces. Midsummer is the Houston Shakespeare Festival. In the Fall is the Houston Jazz Festival.

One of the biggest events at the Miller Outdoor Theater is Cinco de Mayo, May 5th.

Also offering fireworks for the 4th of July celebration as part of the Houston Symphony Fourth of July Concert.

Some performances require tickets for the seating. Tickets are free and are given out 4 per person from 11:00 am to 1:00 pm the day of the event. Any remaining tickets are handed out one hour before the performance. The lawn area never requires tickets.

Plan to come early and either sit down front in seats or bring a blanket, a cooler of food, and enjoy the events from the hill. Remember the bug spray. I recommend getting tickets for seating. (You will have a better chance of seeing and hearing the performance)

Directions

Located in Hermann Park. From 288, exit North MacGregor and go west. You will enter Hermann Park. Continue in the right hand lane as street divides. Turn right on Golf Course Drive. Watch for theater.

Houston Has Talent

RADIO MUSIC THEATER

2623 Colquitt
713-522-7722

Comedy we can identify with

Comedy at its finest. Laugh at Houston. Laugh at Texans. You'll laugh so hard it's guaranteed to hurt. Ever hear of Dumpster, Texas? Ever wondered what would happen if a Category Five hurricane hits Houston? Imagine two Midwesterners' views on "Unconventional Behavior" at the Republican Convention here in 1992. Meet characters like Allen Parkway, (name of a major downtown street), or Kathy Whitmire, our former mayor.

Hours

Thurs - Fri	8:30 pm
Saturday	8 pm & 10:30 pm

Box office opens

Tues - Sat	11 am - 7 pm

Most Shows Sell Out! Reservations Required.

Cost

Per Person	$15

Two-act comedies put on by three people playing multi-characters. Written by one of the owners. It will be the funniest thing you'll ever see. And best yet, shows are written for the general public. Take guests. Relatives. Older kids. Can't say enough. Must-see. Dress is upscale casual.

Directions

From the 59 Freeway, take the Kirby exit towards downtown (north). Go through the 1st light (Richmond) and take the next left. Will be on the left.

Houston Has  *Talent*

RICE UNIVERSITY
RICE PLAYERS

P.O. Box 1892, Houston TX
713-521-PLAY (information)
713-527-4668

Offering great drama

Theatrical classics, Shakespeare, and new works. Offering 4 shows a year. Generally, plays are of high quality. Be on their mailing list or call their recording for the next show. Held in the Hammon Hall on campus.

ALL SHOWS START AT 8:00 PM

General Admission At The Door

Students $4
Seniors $4
Adults $8

Show season generally begins in October.
See great drama at very reasonable prices.

Directions

Located on the Rice Campus on Rice Boulevard between Greenbriar and South Main. Use Entrance #14.

THE RIVER PERFORMING AND VISUAL ARTS CENTER

1475 West Gray
Houston 77019
713-520-1220

Performances by children with special needs

If you are one of the many families having children with special needs, you know finding fun family activities involves a whole new twist. The River Performing and Visual Arts Center got its start when a four-year-old with mild cerebral palsy wanted to take dance just like her older sisters. After much difficulty in trying to find a place that would accept her, her mother started her own performing arts center.

Here they offer dance, art, music, and even drama classes for children with disabilities or chronic illness, ages 3 - 19. Classes for children with special needs are taught by some of the best instructors — from the High School of Performing Arts, the Houston Grand Opera, and the University of Houston's School of Theater. Siblings are welcome, too. No child will be turned away.

Students perform in delightful dramas and recitals; open to the public. Ask about their outreach programs, summer camps, winter and fall semester classes, and other activities.

Hours
Call for class and performance schedules

Cost
Tickets for performances $15

Directions
Located near downtown

SHAKESPEARE BY THE BOOK FESTIVAL

George Memorial Library
1001 Golfview
Richmond, 77469
281-341-2678 • 281-341-2611

Watch annual summer performances of Shakespeare

Watch **A Midsummer Night's Dream**, midsummer (July) at the George Memorial Library's outdoor theater. Shakespeare's plays delight audiences here every summer. Sponsored by the Friends of the Fort Bend Library and other donors. Plays begin at 8 pm. They run one some- times two weekends. Call for more details. A must-see this summer.

Cost

Free

Directions

Take the Southwest Freeway south (across the Brazos River) to exit 762. Go right on FM 762 one mile. The library will be on the right corner of Gulfview and FM 762 (Thompsons High- way)-at the first stop light.

Houston Has 𝄞 Talent

STAGES REPERTORY THEATRE

3201 Allen Parkway Suite #101
713-527-8243

Some of the most exciting theater available

Second largest in Houston and may well be the best. Great children's plays.

Offering "Early Stages" with plays for the younger ones in mind. Like Velveteen Rabbit, Pecos Bill, and Sleeping Beauty. Performances for school groups during the week at 9:30 am and 11:30 am. On Saturday the plays are at 11:30 am and 2:30 pm. Anyone can join a school group during the week if space is available.

Offering "Main Stages" for adults. With performances Wed. through Sat. at 8 pm, and 3 pm on Sunday.

Lots of special privileges go with having a season pass, such as buying extra tickets at half price and getting your choice of seating. Professional actors and actresses are used for all plays. Kids get special attention. Adults are seated on the ends of rows so children can see the play easier. Whether you subscribe for the season or want to enjoy a single event, Stages is great.

Directions

From the 610 West Loop, exit Woodway/Memorial. Go east on Memorial. Follow to Waugh. Go south over Allen Parkway. Go west on D'Amico. Go one block and turn right on Rosine. Will be in the middle of the block on the left.

THEATRE UNDER THE STARS

2600 Southwest Freeway
713-558-2600
Box Office: 713-558-8887

Featuring Broadway musicals

This outstanding non-profit organization brings our country's most popular touring shows to Houston. Theater Under The Stars started in the Miller Outdoor Theater and expanded to the Theater District. Still popular are their summer performances of major productions at the Miller Outdoor Theater. Performances at the Miller Outdoor Theater are free. Call for their schedules.

Tickets can be purchased at their Theatre Under The Stars Box Office which is located at 2600 Southwest Frwy.

Locations of performances vary. Call for further information.

UNIVERSITY OF HOUSTON'S WORTHAM THEATRE

4800 Calhoun
713-743-2929

Great drama at bargain prices

As good as what you see downtown without the price. Offering all kinds of different plays. Be sure to attend their Children's Theater Festival in the summer. They also sponsor the Houston Shakespeare Festival. Call to see what's playing and for their schedule.

Cost

Adult Shows

Students $7
Seniors $7
General $9

Children's Shows

Adults $5.50
Children $4.50

A Season Subscription is $40 for General Admission, $24 for Students and Seniors.

Performing 2 to 3 plays a semester. Reserved tickets must be picked up 24 hours in advance. Tickets purchased by Visa or Mastercard can be picked up at the door, but there will be a handling charge of $1 per ticket. Checks are also accepted.

Directions

Located near downtown on the University of Houston's Campus. From the 59 Freeway, exit I-45 going south. Exit Cullen Avenue. Go past Elgin Avenue. Take the 1st entrance on the left which is Entrance #16. Park in the 1st parking lot on the right. The Wortham Theater will be right there.

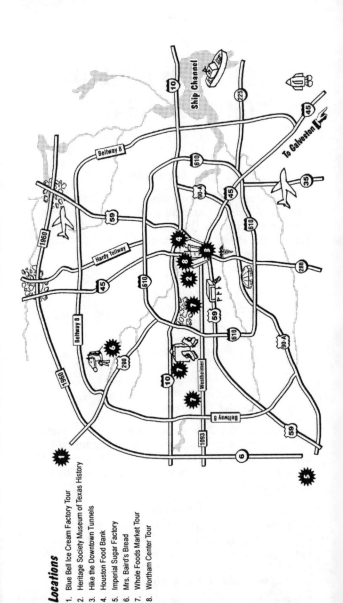

Locations

1. Blue Bell Ice Cream Factory Tour
2. Heritage Society Museum of Texas History
3. Hike the Downtown Tunnels
4. Houston Food Bank
5. Imperial Sugar Factory
6. Mrs. Baird's Bread
7. Whole Foods Market Tour
8. Wortham Center Tour

Chapter 5
TOURS AND MORE

Tours And More

BLUE BELL ICE CREAM FACTORY TOUR

1101 South Horton
Brenham TX 77833
800-327-8135

See how Blue Bell makes their ice cream

Take a tour of their Ice Cream Factory. See how it's made. Open year round. Call for times, schedule varies. No tours on weekends or holidays. Reservations required for groups larger than 15. Tour lasts approximately one hour with your choice of ice cream at the end.

Their cute gift shop, the Country Store (open March through December between 9 am and 3 pm), is open on Saturdays even though the plant is closed.

Hours

Monday through Friday, Closed Saturday and Sunday
Tours begin ...... 10, 11, 1:30, 2, and 2:30
Winter production schedule varies, call before going.

Cost

Children under 6	Free
Children ages 6-14	$1.50
Seniors	$1.50
Adults	$2

Great activity to do one day to get away. In March and April, take the back roads and see the bluebonnets. Washington County Bluebonnet Trail Maps are available from the county's Chamber of Commerce in Brenham. Call 888-Brenham.

Directions

Take Highway 290 west towards Brenham.
Exit FM 577. Will be two miles on the right.

HERITAGE SOCIETY MUSEUM OF TEXAS HISTORY

1100 Bagby
713-655-1912

Sam Houston Park is dedicated to Houston's past

Nestled below great skyscrapers are some of Houston's oldest structures; historical homes, restored and furnished in the fashion of their day. Located in a park, dedicated to the great man who led the Texas rebellion and is our city's namesake. Tours begin every hour. Reservations are required for groups larger than 10.

Hours

Open daily except major holidays

Mon - Sat .... 10 am - 4 pm
Sunday .... 1 pm - 4 pm

Tour Cost

Children under 6 .... Free
Children ages 6-12 .... $2
Children ages 13-17 (seniors) $4
Adults $6

Tour office is at 1100 Bagby. Also visit their cute shop that sells Texas souvenirs, crafts, and cookbooks. Shop hours are the same as the tour hours.

Directions

Located downtown on Bagby.

Tours And More

HIKING THE DOWNTOWN HOUSTON TUNNEL SYSTEM
You will find the Tunnel an interesting place to explore

Downtown Houston's 6.3-mile, brightly lit, air conditioned, underground walking system is simply called the
Tunnel. The Tunnel connects over 55 office buildings, ho-
tels, a shopping mall, parking garages, restaurants, banks,
the Theater District, and much more.

Only one building, Wells Fargo Plaza, allows you direct
access from the street to the Tunnel. You can also enter
the tunnel from stairs, escalators, or elevators located inside any buildings connected with the tunnel. Maps of the
Tunnel System are available from the Downtown District.
713-650-3022. The Tunnel is open 7 am - 6 pm Monday
through Friday.

Here are some interesting points. For a great view, take
the elevators to the 60th floor sky lobby of The Texas
Commerce Tower. In Shell One Plaza visit a free museum:
Shell and the American Landscape, 9:30 - 4:30 M-F 713-
241-4900.

DISCOVER HOUSTON TOURS
713-222-Walk (9255)

TunnelWalks through the Houston Downtown Tunnel
System are offered Monday through Friday. Call for rates,
schedules, reservations, and information for these tours.

HOUSTON FOOD BANK

3811 Eastex Freeway, Houston, TX 77026
Ph:713-223-3700

Visit this huge facility that distributes food to our hungry

Ramble along aisles of boxes stacked to the ceiling in storage rooms the size of foot-ball fields and you have some idea of the magnitude of food this incredible place distributes to the hungry in Texas. You will see giant coolers preserving tons of fresh fruits and vegetables from local produce markets, like stacks of bagged potatoes just arriving but soon to be delivered to one of the 400 charitable institutions the Houston Food Bank supplies.

Since the Food Bank's opening, 15 years ago, it has been industriously distributing over a 160 million pounds of food to agencies feeding over 200,000 people a month. Regular staff and volunteers busily unload, sort, and repackage food donated on a regular basis by 500 local businesses.

You will learn fascinating facts on how this fantastic system of networking feeds so many so well as you tour this no-frills facility. Tours last approximately 30 minutes, but better yet, every 1st and 3rd Saturdays are family Saturdays, where your family can come and volunteer. Anyone ages 8 years or older can contribute their time. Hours for this activity are 8 am - noon and training simply takes 30 minutes.

Call to arrange a time to tour the facility.

You will be surprised at what takes place at the Houston Food Bank and will gain an appreciation for the great effort that goes on in our community to feed the hungry. Be sure to wear casual and comfortable shoes and clothes.

Open Tuesday 6-9 pm for volunteers - must be 8 or older.

Directions - From the 59 Freeway

Southbound: Exit Collingsworth, (after after 610), and go right. Go right on Jensen. Go through Cavalcade and take a right on Vintage. The Houston Food Bank parking lot will be on the right.

Northbound: Take the first exit after crossing over I-10, Cavalcade/Collingsworth/Quitman. Get into the right hand lane and make a left on Cavalcade. Make a right on Jensen. Go right on Vintage and watch for parking lot.

IMPERIAL SUGAR FACTORY

8016 90 A, Sugar Land
281-491-9181

See how cane sugar is made

How sweet this one is. Second largest cane sugar factory in the United States. Started in 1843 with a land grant from Stephen F. Austin. See how raw sugar shipped by rail cars from Galveston becomes the sugar we buy at the supermarket.

Great tour. Can't say enough about it. Lasts one hour. Very educational. Interesting. Must call for reservations. Ask for the tour director. Plan to go when weather is cool.

Tour Hours

Weekdays . . . . 10 am & 2 pm
Cub Scout and Girl Scout tours
Closed Holidays

Cost

Free

Wear casual comfortable clothes and shoes. Will be climbing lots of stairs. Very friendly tour guides. Not recommended for small children. Free sugar samples given out at the end. Very safety minded. Leave all jewelry at home. Watches go in pockets!

Directions

Located in Sugar Land. From Highway 6 South, go east on 90 A approximately 2 miles. Turn left on Ulrich, cross over the tracks, watch for Tour Center.

From the 59 Freeway going southwest, take the Sugar Land exit and turn right. Stay to the right as the road (spur 41) curves around to 90 A. Go left on 90 A. Factory will be approximately 2 miles on the right. Cross over the tracks on Ulrich and watch for the Tour Center.

MRS. BAIRD'S BREAD

6650 N. Houston Rosslyn
713-996-5016

See how Mrs. Baird's bread is made

Nine thousand loaves baked daily. More around the holidays. See what Ninnie Baird started from her kitchen in 1908. Still family owned and operated. Today there are twelve such bakeries serving millions of Texans.

See how all this bread is made. Fantastic tour. Can't say enough. Educational. Inspirational. Great for any children's groups, relatives, and family members. A must-do.

Hours

Tours only by reservations.

Cost

Free

Tour lasts one hour. Hot bread and butter with orange juice at the end. More goodies before you leave.

Directions

From the 610 West Loop, exit Freeway 290 going west. Exit Bingle and go right to Behan. Go right. Behan is a short street with Mrs. Baird's at the end.

WHOLE FOODS MARKET TOUR
2900 South Shepherd
713-520-1937

Health food market with lots of atmosphere

Paradise for anyone who likes to cook (or eat). Influenced by the 60s but in pace with the 90's. More than a health food store. Spices, spices, and more spices. Ever heard of mugwart? Rice, beans, nuts, vinegars, mushrooms, herb teas, and much more. Wonderful! Natural! Exotic!

Great sandwiches and salads available in the deli as well as freshly baked items from their bakery. Most of their fresh produce is organically grown.

Ask about a store tour. Children's group tour available. Plan to browse. Have lunch. Known for having great customer service. Their informed staff will answer any questions. There are two other locations. The store on South Shepherd has more atmosphere. Take the whole family to the Whole Foods Market.

Hours
Daily . . . . 9 am - 10 pm
Closed Thanksgiving and Christmas

Two More Locations
6401 Woodway   11145 Westheimer
713-789-4477   713-784-7776

Directions
For the store on South Shepherd, take the South Shepherd/Greenbriar exit from the 59 Freeway. Take South Shepherd North (one-way street). Go through two lights. Will be on the left.

WORTHAM CENTER THEATRE TOUR

500 Texas, Houston
713-546-0281

See Houston's finest theater

Cost $70 million in the making, 437,000 square feet. Built with two theaters for the Houston Opera and the Houston Ballet. This 45-minute tour will impress anyone with this great performing arts center. Operated by volunteers. One of the best tours to go on. Take the family. Make it part of your visit downtown to see the tunnels. Be sure to go here.

Hours

Tours by reservation only, call in advance.

Cost

Free

See backstage, the green room, and other places not seen by the public except on this tour. Very nice. Interesting. Makes going to the opera more exciting.

Directions

Located downtown in the Theater District.

Locations

1. Azalea Trail
2. Bluebonnet Trails
3. Chappell Hill Festivals
4. The Christmas Revels
5. Christmas Tree Farms
6. Fort Bend Cultural Arts Council
7. Houston's Thanksgiving Parade
8. International Festivals
9. The International Quilt Festival
10. The Nutcracker Market
11. Sugar Festival
12. Texas Renaissance Festival

Chapter 6
WATCH FOR THESE ANNUAL EVENTS

THE AZALEA TRAIL

713-523-2483 (Info)

See classic homes, beautiful yards and gardens

A Houston tradition for nearly 64 years. As the azaleas bloom, River Oaks opens its doors to the public.

Visit the River Oaks Garden Club at 2503 Westheimer. Always a part of the event. See fantastic azaleas. The colors. Experts help you grow your own.

Best of all, tour the garden of all gardens. See the Hogg Estate, the Gardens of Bayou Bend. The tour is held two weekends in March, watch newspaper for dates. Homes differ every year. You can pay individual prices for single events.

Cost

Tickets purchased before event $12
Tickets at the door $15
Tickets for individual events $3
Children under 12 . . . . Free

Sponsored as a fundraiser by the River Oaks Garden Club. Purchase tickets at Randalls or Teas Nursuries. Printed map of tour comes with ticket.

Not recommended for small children. Wear comfortable shoes. Lots of walking. Soft drinks can be purchased along the way.

BLUEBONNET TRAILS

Information for seeing the bluebonnets

Grab the camera. Get the kids. It is wildflower time again in Texas. The wildflowers are incredible. Wait until you see a field of bluebonnets. Depending on the weather, wildflowers' peak display is generally in mid—March or early April.

Wildflowers are big business bringing lots of money to Texas. Here is a list of places to call for information.

Call **The Texas State "Weekly Wildflower Report,"** 512-832-7125, and listen to where they are in bloom.

The Texas Travel Information Center Information Hot Line: 800-452-9292.

Bluebonnet Backroad Tour of Colorado County. Tour routes available from the **Columbus Area Chamber of Commerce**. Maps to see the bluebonnets are available. Call 409-732-5135.

Washington County Bluebonnet Trail free maps & updates (information on Bluebonnet Festival in Chappell Hill) are available from the county's Convention & Visitors Bureau in Brenham. Call 800-225-3695 or 888-Brenham.

CHAPPELL HILL FESTIVALS

For more information call
800-225-3695 or 409-836-6033

Don't miss these annual events

BLUEBONNET FESTIVAL

The official Bluebonnet Festival of Texas held each year the 1st or 2nd weekend of April. A very popular event, involving over 125 craft booths and plenty of good food. Hayride tours around town. Visit their historical museum, church, drug store, general store, and rock store. Special fun for the kids. Antiques and collectibles featured, too.

SCARECROW FESTIVAL

The Scarecrow Festival is held the 2nd week of October with 45,000 to 50,000 attending. Well organized with plenty of parking. Offers 125-150 craft and food booths. See demonstrations of broom, pottery, and lace making. Yards of the town folks are decorated with scarecrows. Go on the scarecrow tour, maps provided. This is also part of the Chappell Hill Historical Society's fundraising efforts. Hayride and tours of historical buildings. Lots of fun.

Directions

Chappell Hill is located 63 miles (about 60 minutes) northwest of Houston on 290 (halfway between Hempstead and Brenham).

THE CHRISTMAS REVELS

P.O. Box 271765
Houston, 77277-1765
713-668-3303

A multicultural Christmas production

What is it? It's a colorful costumed theatrical production with music, dance, poetry, drama, and children's songs. Every production is a blend of Anglo-American traditions with those of other cultures from around the world. Everyone participates, both audience and performers. Weekend and weekday performances, seven shows in all. Held in December at the Moores Opera House on the University of Houston's campus. Very enjoyable.

Purchase tickets by mail, over the phone, from Ticketmasters 713-629-3700 or at Foleys or Fiesta stores. Or buy tickets at the box office one hour before performance. Performances do sell out.

Hours

Call for this year's performance schedule

Cost

Adults $20
Children under 12 . . . . $10

Directions

The Moores Opera House is located on the University of Houston's campus. From the 59 Freeway, exit I-45 going south. Exit Cullen Avenue and go right (west) to Entrance #16. Turn left.

CHRISTMAS TREE FARMS

Choose and cut your own Christmas tree from any of these farms. Make this an annual family outing. These farms open the day after Thanksgiving, offer lots of country fun, and feature high-quality Virginia pines.

A Christmas Carole Tree Farm

22254 FM 1486 North, Montgomery 77356

409-449-6747

Choose from over a thousand trees, 6 to 8-feet tall. The farm offers hayrides in Santa's wagon, picnic tables, a swing out by the lake, and hot cider. Bring the dog.

Directions: Located 21 miles west of Conroe. Take Highway 105 west to 1486 and go 7 miles north.

El Kay Farms

60 Kinkaid East, Montgomery 77356

713-899-2341 or 409-597-6107

Not only can you choose and cut your own Christmas tree, you can also enjoy walking the nature trails, taking a hayride, feeding the fish, or picnicking.

Directions: From I-45 North, take 1488 west. Go 15 miles to FM 149 and go north 2 miles. Watch for sign. Will be on the right.

Underwood Farms

P.O. Box 933, Willis 77378

409-856-6465

Hot chocolate, fresh Christmas wreaths and poinsettias add to the fun at this farm. Take a hayride out to choose your tree. You'll find nature trails and a picnic area.

Directions: From I-45 North, exit FM 3083 and go right. Then go left on 1484 past FM 2432 and turn left on Rose Road-the second flashing light. Will be one mile on the left.

FORT BEND CULTURAL ARTS COUNCIL

2601 Cartwright Road Suite F
Missouri City, 77459
281-261-7934

Free annual summer concerts in the park

Add this to your list of fun things to do this summer. Enjoy a concert in the park every Friday night, starting in June. Concerts begin at 7 pm and feature a wide range of music: country western, Cajun, classical, blues, and folk. Sponsored by private and public donations, the concerts are free and open to the public. Bring your lawn chairs, blankets, coolers, and picnics goodies. Concessions are available. Remember the bug spray. Concerts last until dark, eight in all-running through July.

The Fort Bend Cultural Arts Council offers activities such as theatre productions, festivals, and cultural events. Ask to be on their mailing list. Great family outings.

Office Hours
Mon. - Fri. . . . . 9am - 5 pm
Cost
Free
Directions
Locations vary, call for directions.

HOUSTON'S THANKSGIVING PARADE

For more information call
713-654-8900

Houston has that holiday spirit

As Macy's does in New York. Bank United does in Houston, ushering in the Christmas spirit and holiday season. Something great to do while the Thanksgiving turkey cooks.

One of Houston's best loved traditions. The parade begins at 9 am downtown. Watch the newspaper for more details.

See many a marching band. Hundreds in costumes. Beautiful professional floats. Last but not least is the float with Santa Claus.

Hours

Parade starts . . . . 9 am

INTERNATIONAL FESTIVALS
GREEK FESTIVAL
3511 Yoakum   713-526-5377

Be sure to go to the Greek Festival every year

Great way to enjoy Greek culture here in town. Greek food, dancing, travel movies, and booths. Also, tour the beautiful Greek Cathedral. Held in October, on church grounds next to the University of St. Thomas campus. Huge crowds. Educational. Admission is $2.00 for adults, kids are free. Call for date and time.

Directions

Located one block west of Montrose between Westheimer and West Alabama.

THAI FESTIVAL
6007 Stindle   281-820-3255

One of my favorite things to do

I have a friend from Thailand who introduced me to the Thai culture. This is a wonderful annual festival, we go as a family. Some of the best food (maybe strange-looking) you will ever try. Held in April (April 10 & 11, 1999) & October as a fundraiser for their Buddhist temple. Also enjoy the entertainment. I recommend this. Call for date of event.

Directions

From 290, exit Antoine and go north. Antoine is just outside the 610 Loop. Stay on Antoine for several miles, until you come to Breen. The festival will be on the northeast corner of the intersection behind a tall fence. Go through the intersection and look for a gate on the right. Someone will be there to direct you for parking.

119

OTHER FOOD FESTIVALS

Don't miss. Sometimes festivals occur on the same weekend. Simply plan to eat lots of tasty ethnic foods. Great Saturday activity for the families. Watch for dates and times or call these numbers. Think April and October for festivals.

Asian Festival
713-861-8270

The two-day festival in October features arts and craft from Japan, Vietnam, China, Korea, India, Pakistan, Bangladesh, Cambodia, Indonesia, and other areas. See entertainment on four stages: martial arts, classical and folk dances. Sample Thai, Filipino, Japanese, and other Asian foods. Free admission. Opens Sat. Noon-9pm, Sun Noon-dusk.

Festa Italiana
713-524-4222

One weekend in October, attend this downtown food festival, celebrating Houston's Italian community. Eat food from many local Italian restaurants: Butera's, Carmelo's, Carrabba's, Mandola's Deli. Features music, entertainment, pasta-eating contests, vendors, and a children's area. Sat. 11-11, Sun. 11-6. Admission $5. Children 15 and under free. (Hermann Square at City Hall)

Turkish Festival

A smaller downtown festival, with bazaar held one Saturday in October at Jones Plaza (Texas and Smith Streets.) Simply go for the Turkish foods. Admission $2. Opens at 10am.

Japan Festival
713-963-0121

Held annually in Hermann Park's beautiful Japanese Gardens the 2nd weekend of April. Over 20,000 attend. See traditional and folk dance and music. Watch martial art, Ikeban flower design, origami, and calligraphy demonstrations. Buy food prepared by local Japanese restaurants. Free admission. Sat./Sun. 10 am - 6 pm.

THE INTERNATIONAL QUILT FESTIVAL

281-496-1366

Largest quilt show in the nation

Houston's very fortunate. Any quilter's heaven. Great, innovative ideas for quilts, clothing, and accessories. Excellent classes. Beautiful quilts. New trends and styles.

Generally held the last of October or in November, for 4 days. Call **Great Expectations**, a wonderful fabric shop to get the dates. Shop located at 14090 Memorial Drive in Houston.

Thursday tends to be crowded as bus loads of women arrive from everywhere. Many want to be there the first day to buy from the booths. Friday evening tends to slow down.

Food sold but expensive with huge lines. There are tables to sit at. We suggest bringing Randall's great "Antones" deli sandwiches.

Most years the show is held inside the George R. Brown Convention Center on the 59 Freeway, near downtown.

THE NUTCRACKER MARKET

713-523-6300 ext 271

A pre-Christmas event featuring unique gift ideas

Benefitting the Houston Ballet Academy. River Oaks style flea market. Fancy and expensive items. Dress up to go. Great to see with friends or family members. Bring plenty of cash. Will wrap packages and mail gifts. Every year is a new experience.

Held in the Astrohall one weekend in November. The 1999 market will be November 11-14.

Cost

Admission $8
Children under 5 .... free
Parking $5

Directions

In the Astrohall. From the 610 South Loop, exit Kirby. Go north.

SUGAR FESTIVAL
...CELEBRATING THE SWEET LIFE
P.O. Box 110, Sugar Land, 77487-0110

A community celebration featuring activities and entertainment for the whole family

Spice up your Labor Day weekend plans. A major new festival, launched in 1998, promises to be even bigger and better in its up coming years. The festival gate admission is one of the best entertainment values in the state. Once inside the festival grounds, visitors may enjoy major national acts on the main stage, and live entertainment on the children's stage and talent show/exhibition stage. Other features include a children's interactive area, an exciting midway and carnival, more than 100 arts and craft booths, and many other special exhibits. For those who hear the dinner bell, a fabulous food court will be available. Each evening, the festival will close with a spectacular fireworks show.

Hours
(Labor Day Weekend)

Friday	6 - 11 pm
Saturday	10 am - 11 pm
Sunday	10 am - 11 pm
Monday	11 am - 6 pm

Cost

Adults	$6
Children ages 4 to 12	$4
Children under 3	$3

Directions
The festival grounds are located on a 40-acre site at the corner of the Southwest Freeway and Highway 6 in Sugar Land.

TEXAS RENAISSANCE FESTIVAL

Plantersville, Texas
800-458-3435 or 281-970-3558

Huge festival held each year west of Conroe

Eat, wander, and enjoy the atmosphere of centuries past in the piney woods west of Conroe. Held in the fall (seven weekends in October and November). See the shows and booths. Great food. Dress in medieval attire. Bring your camera.

Plan to spend the entire day. Wear comfortable shoes. Great to go with spouse or friends. Tickets bought before the event at Randalls are discounted.

Hours

October and November, seven weekends.
Festival opens at 9:00 am until dark, rain or shine.

Cost

Children under 5 . . . . Free
Children ages 5 - 12 . . . . $8.95
Adults $17.95

Groups of 25 or more can get discounts.
Write Texas Renaissance Festival,
Route #2 Box 650, Plantersville, Texas 77363.

Directions

Located in Plantersville, west of Conroe. Take I-45 North to Conroe. Go west on 105 to Plantersville. Take FM 1774 south for six miles to the festival site. Or take I-45 North to FM 1488, turn left on 1488 to Magnolia, then take 1774 north to the festival.

Location

1. A Movable Feast
2. Aquarium
3. The Bagel Manufactory
4. Black Labrador
5. Cheesecake Factory
6. Churrascos
7. Croissant Brioche Cafe & Bakery
8. Garson
9. The Golden Room
10. Goode Company Barbecue
11. India's Restaurant
12. Jags
13. Joe's Barbecue
14. Kim Son
15. La Madeleine
16. Lupe's Tortillas
17. Mission Burritos
18. Rainbow Lodge
19. Rustic Oak Tea Garden
20. Sammy's Lebanese Restaurant
21. Southern Empress Cruises
22. Star Pizza
23. The Swinging Door

Chapter 7
EATING OUT

Eating **Out**

A MOVABLE FEAST

2202 West Alabama
713-528-3585

One of the most innovative vegetarian restaurants

The name of this restaurant suggests a visit. Inspired by Hemingway, you'll find this a moving experience.

Hours

Sunday .... 11 am - 8 pm
Mon. - Sat. .... 9 am - 9 pm

(Also serves tuna and chicken.) Blackboard specials. Friendly.

Directions

Take the 59 Freeway. Exit Kirby and go north. Turn right on W. Alabama. Will be on the corner of W. Alabama and Greenbriar before you get to Shepherd.

AQUARIUM
AN UNDERWATER DINING ADVENTURE

11 Kemah Waterfront, Kemah 77565
281-334-9010

New fun restaurant at the Kemah Waterfront

No dining blahs here. Watch sharks, stingrays, and tropical fish in huge aquariums while enjoying great seafood dishes. The décor includes a 3-story aquarium that will excite any ocean lover. Not into seafood? The restaurant's menu includes sandwiches, salads, beef, chicken, and pasta dishes. Eat out on the patio. The restaurant offers banquet facilities, too. Reservations are accepted for groups with 10 or more.

Best of all, the Aquarium is located at the Kemah Waterfront. Watch ships come and go. The complex now includes retail shops, amusement rides, an interactive dancing fountain, and other restaurants.

Hours

Mon. - Thurs.	5 pm - 10 pm
Friday	5 pm - 11 pm
Saturday	11 am - 11 pm
Sunday	11 am - 10 pm

Cost
$10.99 - 25.99

Directions

From Houston, take I-45 South and exit NASA Road 1. Go east 7 miles to 146 and go south. Crossover the bridge and go left on 6th Street-at the first light. Will be in the Kemah Waterfront Complex.

THE BAGEL MANUFACTORY

2438 Rice Blvd. (At Rice University Village)
713-520-ROLL (7655)

Watch bagels manufactured as you eat

Jalapeno, garlic cheddar, banana nut, strawberry, blueberry, cinnamon raisin, and sesame are just a few varieties of bagels offered: 16 varieties.

Cream cheese spreads with spinach and water chestnut, apricot and peach, garlic and herb. Much, much, more.

More than just bagels. New York Delicatessen Bagel Chips. Best yet. They come in gift boxes and can be sent to clients, friends, and relatives. Place an order. They do catering.

Fun for the family. Great place to get away for a casual lunch with friends or relatives.

Directions

Located in the Rice University Village. Exit Kirby from the 59 Freeway and go south. Turn left on Rice and go 1 block.

BLACK LABRADOR

4100 Montrose
713-529-1199

A little England in Houston

Play chess with life-size pieces out front. Or get cozy in front of the fireplace on a cold day. This English restaurant invites you to relax and enjoy talking. And of course the authentic English food — traditional fish and chips, the Shepherd's Pie, Banger & Mash (with genuine English pork) Bubble and Squeak, and Scotch Beef are to die for. Can't decide? They offer a sample. The menu includes soups, salads, sandwiches, hamburgers, and seafood. Save room for some bread pudding or raspberry trifle. Family friendly and lots of fun.

Hours

Mon. - Sat. . . . . 11 am - 11 pm
Sunday . . . . 11 am - 10 pm

Cost

$7.95 - 13.95

Directions

Located at Montrose and Richmond.

Eating *Out*

CHEESECAKE FACTORY

The Galleria, 5015 Westheimer
713-840-0600

Voted the "best cheesecake in Houston" by The Houston Chronicle

With 49 tasty cheesecakes to choose from, you know you'll be back. Just to mention a few, enjoy fresh strawberry, chocolate raspberry truffle, white chocolate chunk macadamia nut, key lime, brownie sundae, German chocolate, and Oreo flavored cheesecakes. Their specialties include baked goods, pastries, and ice cream delights, too.

Best of all, the Cheesecake Factory stays open late weekday and comes in handy after a play or show. Not only do they serve cheesecake and fine desserts, their menu also offers over 200 entrees: soups, salads, pizza, sandwiches, burgers, chicken, fish, steak, seafood, and pasta dishes. You will find a little of every kind of food. Or simply come for one of their fancy omelets or appetizers.

Enjoy their Sunday brunch-served until 2pm. The Cheesecake Factory will surely be a family favorite.

Hours

Mon. - Thurs. . . . . 11 am - 11 pm
Fri. - Sat. . . . . 11 am - Midnight
Sunday . . . . 11 am - 10 pm

Cost

$8 - $19

Directions

Located at the Galleria, the Cheesecake Factory is situated on ground level between Neiman Marcus and Lord and Taylor department stores, facing Westheimer. Coming from the 610 Loop, it will be past Post Oak Boulevard.

CHURRASCOS

2055 Westheimer/S. Shepherd
713-527-8300

Unique restaurant serving cuisine from the American Continents

The place to go for a special occasion. But we recommend not waiting. Any excuse will do. South American cuisine that has to be one of the best places to eat in Houston. Try their beef. Dessert is another wonderful experience. Fried plantains are served with sauces. A must-do. You'll love this one.

Hours
Call for times

Cost
Moderate to expensive

Reservations recommended. See their wall of newspaper clippings. Write-ups about the restaurant from even the *New York Times*.

Owners opened another restaurant called Americas.

Other locations at:
9705 Westheimer/Gessner 713-952-1988
1320 West Bay Area Blvd; Friendswood 77546
281-461-4100

CROISSANT BRIOCHE CAFE AND BAKERY

2435 Rice Boulevard
713-526-9188

Serving the best French food in Houston

You may find it difficult deciding what you want. Many varieties of croissants. (Think of it ... chocolate croissants!) Varieties of danish pastry, quiches, salads, soups, and sandwiches.

The list of wonderful desserts is almost endless. Take anyone along. Fun. Great place to stop in while shopping in the area. Or take home for later. Wonderful breads.

Next door to the Pottery Guild and The Bagel Manufactory. Two blocks away from La Madeleine Restaurant.

Hours

Mon - Sat . . . . 7 am - 7 pm
Sunday . . . . 7 am - 5 pm

Directions

Located in the Rice University Village. Exit Kirby from the 59 Freeway and go south. Turn left on Rice and go 1 block. Will be next to Kinko's on the right.

Eating **Out**

GARSON

2926 Hillcroft
Houston 77057
713-781-0400

Fine Persian cuisine

Have a Middle Eastern food experience-in Houston. Here's the place to eat shish kabobs — in its varieties. Or stews. Try their filet mignon, seafood, and steaks. Large portions, too.

Great appetizers.

Hours
Daily (Sundays 'til 10 pm) .. 11 am - 11 pm

Cost
Lunch $5.95-17.95
Dinner $7.95-18.95

Directions
Located at the corner of Hillcroft and Richmond Streets.

Eating Out

THE GOLDEN ROOM RESTAURANT

Thai and Chinese Cuisine
1209 Montrose Blvd., Houston 77019
713-524-9614

Eat great Thai food at this little restaurant

Just how spicy do you want it? Not that the Chinese food isn't good here, but it's the Thai dishes you must try — hot, medium, or mild — served your way. Choose from their menu a delightful eating adventure that will invite further exploring (half the fun is noticing what others are eating, too). Suggested entrees include their Paht Thai that comes with a wonderful sauce on the side, or the Red Curry, prepared with sliced chicken or beef. But don't stop there, their soups, salads, desserts, and other entrees deserve attention, too.

Hours

Closed Sundays
Lunch
Mon. - Thurs. . . . . 11:30 am - 2:30 pm
Dinner
Mon. - Thurs. . . . . 5 pm - 9:30 pm
Fri. and Sat. . . . . 5 pm - 10:30 pm

Cost
$6.95-11.95

Directions
Located on Montrose Bld. between W. Dallas and W. Gray Streets.

Eating **Out**

GOODE COMPANY BARBECUE

5109 Kirby   713-522-2530
8911 Katy Freeway   713-464-1901

Famous genuine Texas barbecue

For any out-of-town guest wanting to experience the real thing. Everything is made from scratch. This outfit originated 19 years ago on Kirby. Next to their Kirby location is the **Hall of Flame**, a retail store for their barbecue sauce, jalapeno garlic bread, homemade sausage, marinades, and salsa. Plus souvenirs, vintage clothing, Texas memorabilia, and cooking tools.

Hours

Daily . . . . 11 am - 10 pm

Food served cafeteria style, no reservations, and is inexpensive.

Directions

From the 59 Freeway, exit Kirby and go south. Will be on the left. Additional parking is available behind their "Hall of Flame" store.

Also try:
Goode Company Hamburgers and Taqueria
4902 Kirby   713-520-9153

Goode Company Seafood
2621 Westpark   713-523-7154

Eating Out

INDIA'S RESTAURANT

5704 Richmond Avenue
713-266-0131

Restaurant serving authentic cuisine from India

An ethnic adventure in good food. They love to serve the adventuresome who come for their first time. Here in Houston over 10 years.

Hours

Lunch . . . . 11 am - 2:30 pm
Dinner (Fri & Sat until 10:30) . 5:30 pm - 10 pm

Offers a daily lunch buffet.
Their cuisine is from Northern India.

Cost

Lunch Buffet $7.95
Dinner . . . . $6.96 - $13.95

Directions

Located between Chimney Rock
and Fountain View on Richmond.

JAGS

Decorative Center
5120 Woodway
713-621-4765

Enjoy a unique luncheon experience

Lunch at one of Barbara and George Bush's favorites. Eat inside the most unique place to shop for interior décor in Houston. Very different. Wonderful sweet rolls and great food. The friendly servers graciously assists any indecisive patron. Only serving lunch on weekday, call for reservations. A great place to impress a friend. Dressy casual.

Hours
Mon. - Fri. . . . . 11:30 am - 2:30 pm

Cost
$8-13

Directions
Located inside the Decorative Center at the corner of Woodway and Sage.

JOE'S BARBECUE

1400 E. Highway 6
Alvin, Texas
281-331-9626

Authentic Texas Barbecue

We discovered this fantastic place to eat years ago coming back from a day in Galveston. We have since been there often. Our favorite place to get away to talk and eat. A great place to take the entire family or any relative.

Hours

Sun - Thur	11 am - 10 pm
Fri and Sat	11 am - 11 pm

Cost

Inexpensive

Can't say enough for their "all you-can-eat" beef ribs, salad bar, great cobbler and ice cream. Friday and Saturday evenings are generally busy. Service is great and lines move quickly. Offers catering services for any event. Visit their gift and floral shop called the Barnyard Boutique.

Directions

Located about 20 miles south of Sugar Land on Highway 6 in Alvin. Take Highway 6 South. Will be before Bypass 35 on the right.

KIM SON

2001 Jefferson
713-222-2461

Some of the best Vietnamese food in town

Recognized as one of our best restaurants. Their rich flavors of traditional foods such as hot and sour soup and their charcoal-broiled beef are wonderful.

Definitely one of the largest restaurants with their 22,000 square-foot facility. Opening in 1993. Huge menu. Great service. We recommend trying their spring rolls with peanut sauce.

Hours

Mon - Thur ....11 am - 11 pm
Fri and Sat ....11 am - Midnight

Cost

Inexpensive to moderately priced

Family owned and operated. Owners were well established in the restaurant business before coming here as refugees. The La Family was stranded on a Pacific island after pirates robbed them of everything. Immigrating to Houston in 1980, they worked hard to save enough money to open their first Kim Son.

Directions

Located across the 59 Freeway from the George R. Brown Convention Center. Going north on the 59 Freeway toward downtown, exit Gray Avenue. Follow the feeder until you come to Jefferson. Will be on the corner.

Other locations

8200 Wilcrest at Beechnut 713-568-8651
7531 Westheimer 713-783-0054
300 Milan 713-222-2789

LA MADELEINE RESTAURANT
6205 Kirby   713-942-7081

Wonderful authentic French food

Imagine yourself eating lunch in a Paris bistro. Wonderful hot sandwiches and quiches. Bread baked daily in authentic wood-burning ovens. Wonderful smells. Especially the roasting chickens smothered in rosemary and other spices. You will want dessert, so save room. Food is served cafeteria style. Usually a healthy lunch crowd. Service is great. On nicer days eat outside.

Thirteen locations throughout Houston. La Madeleine at 10,001 Westheimer in the Carillon Center has its own grist mill! Sells flour. Caters to parties.

Special occasion orders and cakes. Holiday baking, such as King's Cakes and Buche de Noel cakes for Christmas.

Breads are extra healthy using only four ingredients, no fats. Watch for daily specials. Tour of bakery available.

Hours
Sun - Thur .... 6:30 am - 10 pm
Fri and Sat .... 6:30 am - 11 pm

Directions
On Kirby and University Boulevard in the Rice University Village.

Other Locations
5505-A FM1960, 281-893-0723
4570 Kingwood Dr., 281-360-1681
2675 Town Ctr Blvd., First Colony Mall, 281-494-4401
600 Travis/Commerce Tower, 713-325-6715
4002 Westheimer, 713-623-0645
5015 Westheimer, Galleria, 713-993-0287
10,001 Westheimer, 713-226-7674
929 W. bay Area Blvd., Clear Lake, 281-316-6135
770 W. Sam Houston Prkwy N. Ste 100, 713-465-7370
6500 Woodway, 713-722-8449

Eating Out

LUPE'S TORTILLAS

318 Stafford Street, Houston 77079
281-496-7580

A super family restaurant

Waiting is part of the family fun at Lupe's—even your kids will agree. The huge sandbox out front keeps them happy until you're seated. Once inside, enjoy some of the best Tex Mex cuisine in Houston. You won't go wrong trying their tasty "Chicken Lupe" dish—one of their most popular — or any of their enchilada entrees. Impress your out-of-town relatives and guests with this unique place to eat. Come early. As popular as this restaurant is, reservations aren't taken. Note that Lupe's serves only dinner on Saturdays and Sundays. Wear casual attire.

Hours

Lunch
Mon. - Fri. . . . . 11am - 2pm

Dinner
Sun. - Thurs. . . . . 5:30pm - 8:30pm
Fri. and Sat. . . . . 5:30pm - 9:30pm

Cost
$6.95-12

Directions
Located at Highway 6 and I-10. From Highway 6, go east on the I-10 feeder road and turn right at the second street-Stafford. Will be a Wells Fargo Bank on the corner. From I-10, exit Highway 6 and go south. Turn right on Grisby (shortly on the left, past the fruit stand).

Eating **Out**

MISSION BURRITOS

2245 W. Alabama • 713-529-0535
909 Texas (at Main) • 713-224-1440

Named one of the best cheap eats in Houston

Want a tasty lunch in a jiffy? Mission Burritos' fresh burritos take no time at all to assemble. From an assemble line of fresh ingredients, build your own burrito the way you like it, with rice, beans, lettuce, beans, cheese, mushrooms, sprouts, guacamole, sour cream, char grilled chicken, or beef. These Mexican meals wrapped in huge tortillas will take both hands to handle.

Their menu includes a variety of soups, salads, tacos, desserts, and a kid's meal. Enjoy eating inside or out on the patio under the 100-year-old oak. The patio and enclosed area around the tree make an ideal spot for a birthday party or group lunch. Ask about their catering service.

The Mission Burritos, located downtown in the Rice Hotel, offers a breakfast menu of tacos and burritos. Or stop in after a concert or a play, they're open until 11pm on Fridays and Saturdays.

Hours

W. Alabama
Mon. - Sat. . . . . 11 am - 11 pm
Sunday . . . . 11 am - 10 pm

Downtown
Mon. - Thurs. . . . . 7 am - 10 pm
Friday . . . . 7 am - 11 pm
Saturday . . . . 9 am - 11 pm

Cost (burritos)
$5-8.75

Directions
*Located on W. Alabama between Kirby and Greenbriar Street.
And on Texas Avenue between Travis and Main Street.*

Eating Out

RAINBOW LODGE

1 Birdsall
713-861-8666

A great place to take anyone needing to be impressed

Here you can have a lodge atmosphere serving wild game. Rustic yet romantic. Beautiful grounds.

The dress is coat and tie, but they aren't required. Serving brunch, lunch, and dinner.

Menu includes wild game such as quail, duck, venison, and buffalo as well as seafood, steak, lamb, chicken, and veal. We suggest trying the "Mix Grill" dish so you can sample their different meats. Lunch and brunch $12 - $25. Dinner $16-$35.

Hours

Closed Monday

Lunch

Tues - Fri	11:30 am - 4 pm
Sunday Brunch	10:30 am - 3 pm

Dinner

Tues - Fri	5 pm - 10:30 pm
Saturday	6 pm - 10:30 pm
Sunday	5 pm - 10:30 pm

Directions

Located near Memorial Park. From the 610 West Loop exit Memorial Drive and go east. Stay on Memorial and you will come to Birdsall. Turn right. You will see the restaurant.

RUSTIC OAK TEA GARDEN RESTAURANT

10118 Thurleigh Street
281-495-9272

One of the great places to lunch

You probably have heard how great this place is for lunch. Now they offer dinner, too.

Lunch in a tea room atmosphere with a variety of quiches, salads, finger sandwiches, and crepes served with gourmet teas, coffees, and wines. To follow, there is a selection of delectable desserts.

Dinner has the homemade touch of continental cuisine with the mushroom sauces and stuffed chicken. You will love this place.

Hours
Closed Monday & Sunday
Lunch
Tues - Sat . . . . 11 am - 2 pm
Dinner
Wed- Sat . . . . 5:30 pm - 9:30 pm

Cost
Lunch . . . . $6.95 - $11.95
Dinner . . . . $13.95 - $30

Directions
Located near the Sam Houston Tollway and the 59 Freeway. From the 59 Freeway going north (from Sugar Land), exit the Airport/Kirkwood exit and travel the feeder road to the light at the Sam Houston Tollway. Turn right and then turn right again on Thurleigh. Will be at the end of the (short) street. Southbound on 59, exit the Sam Houston Tollway eastbound. Turn right on Thurleigh.

Eating 🍴 *Out*

SAMMY'S LEBANESE RESTAURANT

5825 Richmond 77057
713-780-0065

Serving authentic Lebanese food

Very authentic. A wonderful lunch experience for anyone who likes adventure. Catering to the first-timer with their "Mezza" plate that lets you sample twelve different foods. Educational.

Hours

Mon -Thur	11 am - 10:30 pm
Fri and Sat	11 am - 11 pm
Sunday	Noon - 10 pm

Very good food and service. If you enjoy cuisines from other countries and a new experience you'll enjoy going here.

Directions

Located on Richmond between Chimney Rock and Fountain View outside the 610 Loop.

Eating 🍴 *Out*

SOUTHERN EMPRESS CRUISES
Highway 105 (Lake View Marina)
Lake Conroe
409-588-3000 or 800-324-2229

Dine on an authentic paddlewheeler on Lake Conroe

You will have to plan ahead to get reservations for this adventure. Take a 2-hour lunch cruise or 3-hour dinner cruise. The boat makes an interesting voyage of the lake, letting you see the beautiful homes. Homes on Lake Conroe are very impressive. Catering their own food, they serve a variety of different things. Friday night is a seafood buffet with prime rib. Enjoy their live entertainment in the Magnolia Room with their band "Southern Nights." You will want to dance the night away. Or go out onto the upper decks and enjoy the cruise from the lounge chairs.

Hours
Call for reservations and times.

Cost
Lunch $20
Dinner $36.50

Directions
Located 40 miles north of Houston. The Southern Empress is located 7.5 miles west of I-45 on Highway 105, between Stromen Realty and Pizza Hut at Lake View Marina.

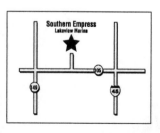

Eating Out

STAR PIZZA

2111 Norfolk, Houston 77007
713-523-0800
140 Heights Avenue, Houston
713-869-1241

Pizza isn't just "fast food" at Star Pizza.

Their pizza specialties give new definition to anything ordinary. Even the word spinach takes on new meaning when it's combined with fresh garlic—in one of their favorites—"Joe's Pizza". The difficulty comes choosing your pizza. Then again enjoy their buffet on weekdays from 11am — 2pm. Other entrees include pasta dishes, salads, and sandwiches. Enjoy casual dining in a whimsical atmosphere.

Hours

Mon. - Thurs. . . . . 11am - 11pm
Fri. and Sat. . . . . 11am - Midnight
Sunday . . . . 11am - 11pm

Cost

$5 -$15.50

Directions

From the 59 Freeway, exit S. Shepherd/Greenbriar. Take S. Shepherd north 2 blocks to Norfolk. Go left. Will be behind the Whataburger.

THE SWINGING DOOR

FM 359, Richmond, Texas
281-342-4758

Famous Texas Barbecue

The place to impress any guest who has never experienced the real Texas. Lots of atmosphere. Famous barbecue, includes Pecan Smoked Beef Brisket. Scenic drive into the countryside.

Hours

Closed Monday and Tuesday

Wed and Thur	11 am - 9 pm
Fri and Sat	11 am - 10 pm
Sunday	11 am - 8:30 pm

Reservations required on weekends

Cost

Inexpensive

Dance to the music of the "Brazos" every Saturday and most Friday nights. $3 with dinner, $4 without.

Directions

Take 90 A west toward Richmond. Before the Brazos River you come to 359. Go right. Approximately 5 minutes on your right.

LATE BITES

Ever looked for a place to eat after a play or show-on a weeknight? The following restaurants keep late hours during the week. Choose from this handy list for a late night meal or dessert. Hours listed are for weekdays only.

Arcodoro-Italian (11pm)
Centre at Post Oak 5000 Westheimer (Post Oak Blvd.)
713-621-6888

Cheesecake Factory-American, bakery (11pm)
5015 Westheimer (Post Oak Blvd.) 713-840-0600

Dolce and Freddo-Desserts, coffees (1am)
5515 Kirby Dr. (Sunset Blvd.) 713-521-3260
7595 San Felipe (west of S. Voss Road) 713-789-0219
5403 W. FM (Champions Dr.) 281-893-4343

Europa Café-International menu (11pm)
2536 Nottingham (Kirby) 713-942-0001

Garson-Persian (11pm)
2926 Hillcroft (Westheimer) 713-781-0400

Hard Rock Café-American (11pm)
2801 Kirby Dr. (Westheimer) 713-520-1134

Mai's-Vietnamese (24 hours)
3403 Milam (Francis) 713-520-7684

Maxim's-French-Continental food, desserts (10:30pm)
3755 Richmond 713-877-8899

Locations

1. Adventure Bay Water Park
2. Aerodrome Ice Skating
3. Alabama & Coushetta Indian Reservation
4. Bananas
5. Celebration Station
6. Challenger Learning Center
7. Del Lago Golf Resort & Conference Center
8. Discovery Zone Fun Centers
9. Funplex Family Fun Mall
10. Gulf Greyhound Racing
11. Laser Quest Houston
12. Laserzone
13. Malibu Grand Prix Raceway & Castle
14. Oil Ranch
15. The Orange Show
16. Plaster Fun House
17. Sam Houston Raceway Park
18. Splashtown USA
19. Texas Rock Gym
20. Texas State Railroad
21. Viking Archery

Chapter 8
AMUSEMENT PARKS & ATTRACTIONS

ADVENTURE BAY WATER PARK

13602 Beechnut
281-530-5979

Water park with activities for any age

Any Houstonian's idea of how to beat the heat. Water activities to keep any age cool. Formerly the Fame City Water Works.

You won't have to ask the kids twice. Attractions like 6 tube slides, the lazy river ride, a giant wave pool, 3 speed slides, a children's area, a gift shop, plus more.

Hours

Mon - Thur .... 10 am - 7 pm
Fri and Sat .... 10 am - 8 pm
Sunday .... 11 am - 7 pm

Cost

Children under 3 .... Free
Children under 48 inches $12.99
Adults/Children over 48 inches .. $16.99

Ask about their Birthday Party Packages. Season passes are available for $55—watch or call for special promotions.

Directions

Go east on Beechnut from Highway 6. Will be about a mile on the left.

AERODROME ICE SKATING

16225 Lexington Blvd., Sugar Land
281-265-RINK (7465)
8220 Willow Place N., Houston
(Near Willowbrook Mall)
281-847-5283

An ice skating facility in Sugar Land

Located in the city of Sugar Land. Home to the Aeros Hockey Team. Offering the finest in public ice skating.

Also figure skating lessons, hockey classes, hockey camps, and party facilities. See their full-service pro shop with official Aeros Hockey Team merchandise and more.

Opening in December of 1995 is a second rink with many new and exciting things offered. Also call and ask when the Aeros will be practicing. The public can watch without charge.

Hours

Call for their schedule.
Times vary according to the Aeros needs.

Cost

General Admission (weekdays) $5
General Admission (weekends) $6
Skate Rental $2.50

Directions

From Houston, take the 59 Freeway south and exit Highway 6. Take Highway 6 south 2 lights and go right on Lexington. The rink will be on the left next to the FBISD Administration Building. (Mercer Field)

ALABAMA AND COUSHATTA INDIAN RESERVATION

Route 3 Box 640, Livingston TX 77351
800-444-3507

Visit an Indian reservation

Get the kids, grab the camera. Be sure to go here. Home of the Alabama and Coushatta Tribes. Offering two bus tours, one walking tour and a ride through the woods on a miniature train. Plus tribal dances. All for one price. Visit their gift shop with Indian handmade crafts and their museum of great artifacts. Restaurant on premises.

Hours

Summer (opening March)

Mon - Sat .... 9 am - 6 pm
Sunday .... Noon - 6 pm
Call — winter times can vary.

Cost

Adults $12
Children ages 4 - 12 .... $10
Children under 4 .... Free

Lakeside campsites are available along with fishing and paddle boat rentals. Very educational.

Directions

Take Highway 59 north to 190 and go east about 17 miles. Will be on the right.

BANANAS

17611 Kuykendahl
Spring 77379
281-370-6499

Activities for small children

Here's a fun place to take the kids. Privately owned, with a personal touch, Bananas is located in a quiet little shopping center, minutes away from the freeway. It offers a clean, well-run, but small establishment for children ages 5 and younger.

Whether it's a private birthday party, exploring music and movement, or playtime, children love coming here. Weekends are reserved for 1.5 hour birthday parties, offering cake, pizza, ice cream, punch, balloons, and more. Guests enjoy time at the fun center. Ask about their morning Kindermusik programs. Play times vary, mostly afternoons. Call before going.

Hours

Mon (Kindermusik) . . . . 10 am - 2 pm
Tues - Fri (Kindermusik) . 9 am - 10:30 am
Sat - Sun . . . . Private Birthday Parties

Cost

Varies with activities
Open Play . . . . $3.75 - $6.75

Directions

From I-45 North, exit FM 1960 and go west. Go right on Kuykendahl. Will be two lights up on the left.

CELEBRATION STATION

6767 Southwest Freeway, 713-981-7888
180 W. Rankin Road, 281-872-7778

A small, well-run amusement park

This noticeably fun-looking place you pass on the Southwest Freeway has lots to offer: batting cages, bumper boats, go carts, miniature golf, pool tables, a smaller child's play area, and an animated show where pizza is served and more. Clean, well run. Recommended for a family activity or a child's birthday party.

Hours

Winter
Mon - Thur . . . . 4 pm - 9 pm
Fri . . . . 4 pm -11 pm
Sat .10 am -11 pm
Sunday . . . . .noon - 9 pm

Summer
Mon - Thur . . . . 11 am - 11 pm
Fri and Sat . . . . 10 am - Midnight
Sun . . . . 11 am - 11 pm

Cost

Each activity is individually priced

Directions

Two locations: Southwest Freeway between Bellaire and Hillcroft and on I-45 North between the 610 North Loop and Beltway 8.

The Houston Museum of Natural Science
CHALLENGER LEARNING CENTER

Brazos Bend State Park
21901 FM 762, Needville
409-553-3400 • 713-639-4629

Experience the thrills and challenges of manning a space flight.

The Challenger Learning Center is dedicated to the brave crew of the Challenger Flight that ended in tragedy. Let your youth group crew a simulated space mission. Two hours long, they will spend one hour aboard the spacecraft and one hour working at consoles in mission control.

Popular with grades 4 -12, the Center offers a Mini Mission for smaller groups and a Junior Mission for younger children in grades 1-3. Missions for adults, too. Call for more details about group sizes and cost.

Ask about the day astronomy classes, featuring hands-on activities with telescopes, spectroscopes, and other interesting astronomy tools. These classes gear to any age level.

See the 36" telescope one of the largest in our nation. Before leaving, be sure to walk the Creekfield Nature Trail. See deer, numerous birds, armadillos, and other wildlife.

Hours
Designed for groups, by reservation only.

Cost
Varies with the different space mission
Per Mission ....$140 - $240

Directions
See directions for Brazos Bend State Park. From the head-quarters, continue through the park two miles. Watch for sign. Park on the left and walk the pathway on the right.

DEL LAGO GOLF RESORT & CONFERENCE CENTER

600 Del Lago Blvd., Montgomery, Texas
800-335-5246
409-582-6100

A resort on Lake Conroe offering family activities

Stay in this beautiful high-rise overlooking Lake Conroe, in one of their lakeside Villas (complete with boat slip) or a Golf Cottage. Offering a large variety of recreational activities for the entire family or a place for restful retreat.

Fun things to do: fishing, waterskiing, parasailing, boating, 18 holes of golf, 11 tennis courts, volleyball, basketball, horseshoes, a sandy beach, racquetball courts, a health spa, elegant dining and dancing. Plan to rent a boat. Offering ski, pontoon, fishing, and party boats.

Lake Conroe is a fantastic 32,000 acre-lake surrounded with pine.

Directions

Located 65 minutes from downtown Houston. Take I-45 north and exit 105. Go west approximately 15 miles to Walden Road and go right. Follow Walden Road to Del Lago. Will be on the right.

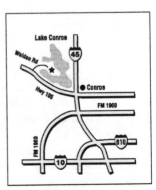

DISCOVERY ZONE FUN CENTER

4016 Bellaire Blvd.
713-667-5437

Activity and fun for children

It's the little things that make the difference. A well-thought-out establishment. Entertainment for anyone under twelve.

Hours

Mon through Thur .... 11 am - 8 pm
Fri and Sat .... 10 am - 9 pm
Sunday .... 11 am - 7 pm

Cost

Under 38" tall $4.99
16 yr or younger $7.99

Stay as long as you want. Food reasonably priced and good quality. Separate glassed-in area with television for adults with total view of your children. Smaller children won't miss out on the fun with their own separate area. Tickets even in small amounts can be redeemed for prizes.

Best of all, well trained baby-sitters will tend your children. The kids can be dropped off for lots of supervised fun on a busy day. Be sure to check this place out.

Other Locations

10201 Katy Freeway, Houston, 713-722-7011
19801 Gulf Freeway, Webster, 281-338-1621
124 E. FM 1960 Bypass, Humble, 281-540-3866
1818 SE Beltway 8, Pasadena, 713-473-0386

FUNPLEX
FAMILY FUN MALL

13700 Beechnut
281-530-7777

Huge complex offering all kinds of amusement activities

A shopping mall turned into fun. Caters to all ages. Offering bumper cars, bowling, indoor miniature golf, roller skating, movies, a play area for the small ones, and arcades and more. Great birthday party room.

Winter Hours

Closed Monday, Tuesday, Wednesday
Call for Spring Break hours

Wednesday & Thursday ... 5 pm - 10 pm
Friday .... 5 pm - Midnight
Saturday .... 11 am - Midnight
Sunday .... 11 am - 10 pm

Summer Hours

Mon through Thurs ...... 11 am - 10 pm
Friday & Saturday ..... 11 am - Midnight
Sunday .... 11 am - 10 pm

Cost

Individual prices for activities,
package rates, and specials.

Directions

Located on Beechnut approximately 1 mile east of Highway 6.

GULF GREYHOUND RACING

1000 FM 2004, La Marque TX
800-ASK-2WIN • 409-986-9500

Wonderful facility for greyhound racing

The world's largest greyhound racing operation. Opened in 1992. During its first year, this park broke the record in the industry for attendance and wagers. It had 2.2 million people visit.

Located south of Clear Lake, this facility has 315,000 square feet with four levels. Their clubhouse seats 1,900. There are 318 teller windows.

Featuring specialty bars, valet parking, full service dining, a lounge and clubhouse. There are closed circuit televisions throughout the complex, making it easy to follow the races. Parking $1, Valet $3.

Hours
Simulcast
Daily . . . . begins 11 am
Post Times
Gates open 1 hour before racing begins
Tues & Thurs . . . . 7:30 pm
Wed . . . . 4 pm & 7:30 pm
Fri, Sat and Sun . . . . . . 1:30 pm & 7:30 pm

Cost
General Admission . . . $1 1st/2nd floors
Clubhouse . . . . $4 3rd/4th floors
Children under 2 . . . . Free 1st/4th floors

Directions
Take I-45 South toward Galveston. Exit #15.
Will be one block west of I-45 South at Exit #15.

LASER QUEST HOUSTON

13711 Westheimer Rd   281-596-9999
6560 FM 1960 West   281-397-6612
100 W. Bay Area Blvd   281-316-3794

Come play this fun game of Laser tag

Imagine yourself wandering through this awesome maze, your heart pounding as you seek out your opponent in this incredible hi-tech game of tag. You're surrounded with action as the fun intensifies. You aim; you fire, you're fired upon.

Your family will find this an unforgettable adventure. Anyone can play the game, who is big enough to wear the laser pack, (children ages 6 or older). Games last approximately 20 minutes.

Laser Quest is a popular activity for birthday parties, corporate groups, clubs, churches, and scout troops, offering team building and customized games.

Hours

Monday's are reserved for private parties

Tue - Thur .... 6 pm - 10 pm
Fri .... 4 pm - midnight
Sat .... 10 am - midnight
Sun .... noon - 10 pm

Cost

Group Discounts available

Non-members .... $ 6.50
Members .... $ 5
Membership $20
Birthday parties per person $11

There are three locations in the Houston area. Remember to wear casual, comfortable clothes and tennis shoes. You will see what computers can do to a simple game of tag.

Directions

Located between Eldridge and Highway 6 on Westheimer. Also located 1 mile east of Willowbrook Mall on 1960, between Champions and Cutten Drive.

LASERZONE

4125 South Highway 6, Sugar Land 77478
281-277-2900

New facility features large area for laser tag

It's the huge, 10,000-square-feet 3 level maze, that is fun at Laserzone. Wander through the maze. Tag your opponent. Score big points — all computerized. You'll enjoy playing this modern game of tag. Popular with every age group (5 and older) including adults and seniors.

Bring your friends; plan to have a party. Groups of 10 or more receive a $1 discount on games. Great for children's birthday parties; their birthday package includes two games per person and use of one of their party rooms. Call for more details, available for lock-ins, corporate events, and fund-raisers, too.

Hours

(opens at 1 pm M-F in the summer)
Mon. - Thurs. . . . . 4 pm - 10 pm
Friday . . . . 4 pm - Midnight
Saturday . . . . Noon - Midnight
Sunday . . . . Noon - 10 pm

Cost

Per game $6.50
Memberships (includes a 2 free games & $1 discount/game) . $25

Directions

Located in Sugar Land. Take the Southwest Freeway south and exit Highway 6 South. Go south 2 miles. Will be on the left.

MALIBU GRAND PRIX

1105 West Loop North
713-683-8255

Miniature golf at its finest!

Largest in Houston offering four 18-hole courses. Combine this activity with those at the Grand Prix and you've got a great afternoon or evening of fun.

Summer Hours

Call for winter hours

Mon - Thur	11 am - 10 pm
Fri and Sat	11 am - midnight
Sunday	4 pm - 10 pm

Cost

Activities individually priced or ask for their specials like the Fun Pass or the Bucket of Tokens. Packages offered. Group rates available.

Offering bumper boats, 9 batting cages (with 3 slow pitch). Three sizes in racing cars. Mini racing cars for children ages 7-8. Game room. Full service snack bar.

A Houston establishment for 25 years. The miniature golf Castle has a fantasy atmosphere. Great service. Clean, well-run.

Directions

Located on the west side of the 610 North Loop Feeder. Coming from the south on 610, exit #18. Go under the freeway, back onto the freeway and exit Old Katy Road.

Coming from the north on 610, exit Old Katy Road. Entrance will be at the end of the exit ramp.

OIL RANCH

1 Oil Ranch Road, Hockley, Texas
281-859-1616

A great place to have fun with the kids. A real working ranch where you can be a cowpoke for the day. Featuring pony riding, cow milking, many petting zoos, a hayride, a train ride, miniature golf, swimming, a hay barn, a big lake with paddle boats, and much more. Plenty of activity in a well-run, safety-minded, beautiful facility. Open all year round but some days they are closed.

Hours

Call for a reservation, (hours are seasonal)
Closed Monday. Some Sundays are exclusive.

Tues - Fri .... 10 am - 4 pm
Saturday .... 10 am - 6 pm
Sun (summer only) .... 11 am - 6 pm

Cost

24 months and older $7.99
Groups of ten or more ... $7 Weekends
$5 Weekdays

Great for children. Concession stands available or bring your lunch. Lunches can be eaten in one of the many large pavilions (if not reserved) or in any picnic area. Wear comfortable shoes and play clothes. Remember the swim suits, towels, and sun screen. We recommend a jug of ice water. Water fountains are available. This is a must-do.

Directions

From the 610 West Loop take 290 west to Hockley. In Hockley, go right on Hegar. Go approximately 5 miles and go right on Magnolia Road. Continue for 1 1/2 miles and watch for signs. Will be on the left.

THE ORANGE SHOW

2401 Munger
713-926-6368

Retired postman turns residential property into an amusement park

See what a retired postman did with objects found from his mail route. Obsessed with what he believed to be the perfect food. This man, Jeff McKissack turned his neat little residential property into a bizarre and wonderful tribute to the orange. Colorful, 25 years in the making. A work of art that's very unconventional.

Hours

(Closed Mid-December through Mid-March)
Spring and Fall
Sat and Sun . . . . .noon - 5 pm
June, July, and August
(Closed Monday and Tuesday)
Wed - Fri . . . . 9 am - 1 pm
Sat and Sun . . . . Noon - 5 pm

Cost

Adult & children over 12 . . . .$1

Directions

Located a few minutes south of downtown Houston. Take I-45 south towards Galveston. Go past the University of Houston. Exit Telephone Road. Take the right lane of the feeder and go right on Munger. Will be on the left.

PLASTER FUN HOUSE

777-A Dairy Ashford
281-496-5618

A place where children can have lots of fun

Imagine a place where you can choose from hundreds of pieces of plaster craft to paint and decorate your way. That is what the Plaster Fun House is like. Very popular with any elementary-age children.

Plan to spend the afternoon creating your own masterpiece. You will want to come again and again.

Reservations are welcome. So are walk-ins. A great place to have a birthday party or to take a field trip. Remember to wear older, comfortable clothes.

Winter Hours

Mon - Sat .... 10 am - 6 pm
Sunday .... noon - 5 pm
(Winter hours - Closed on Tuesday)

Summer Hours

Mon - Sat .... 10 am - 6 pm
(Closed on Sunday)

Cost

Per child .... $6 & $7 (plus tax)

Directions

The Plaster Fun House is located on Dairy Ashford south of I-10. From I-10, exit Dairy Ashford. Watch for Perthshire Street. Once you pass Perthshire, it will be on the right in the Ashford Shopping Center.

SAM HOUSTON RACE PARK

7575 North Sam Houston Parkway West, 77064
800-807-RACE (8700) or 281-807-7223

Horse racing facilities in Houston

Opening in 1994, this huge new beautiful facility is located off the Sam Houston Tollway. Offering track-view dining in the Winner's Circle Restaurant with seating for 600 people.

Families are welcome. Children under 12 years of age are admitted free. Parking $2., Valet $5.

Hours

Post times

Thur, Fri, and Sat . . . . 7 pm
Sunday . . . . 5 pm

Cost

General Admission $3
Children under 12 . . . . Free
Seniors $1

Directions

Located on the Sam Houston Tollway between 290 and Windfern/Fallbrook. Take the Windfern/Fallbrook exit. If southbound, make a U-turn under the freeway.

SPLASHTOWN USA

21300 I-45 North
281-355-3300
www.splashtown.com

Largest water park in Houston

More than 40 water slides and 46 acres make it the largest water park in Houston. No better place to spend a hot Houston day. Great for the entire family. Thunder Run is new for 1999.

Hours

Open April 17 - Sept 26 ... 10 am - 8 pm

Cost

Children under two .... Free
Anyone under 48' $13.99
Seniors .... $9.99 with paying guest
Adults $19.99
Individual passes $44.99
Families of Three $119.99

Ask about their season passes. They have a Sunset Super Saver ($12.99) that begins at 4:30. Watch for discount coupons in newspaper. Parking is $3. Picnic area outside park near main gate. Food cannot be brought in. Food sold inside. Season passes are also good for Splashtown in San Antonio.

Directions

Located on I-45 North about 10 miles north of Beltway 8. From I-45 North, exit Louetta/FM 2920.

TEXAS ROCK GYM

9716 Old Katy Road #102, Houston TX 77055
201 Hobbs Rd., Ste. #1, League City TX 77573
281-338-7625 Web Site: www.texrockgym.com

A state-of-the-art climbing facility

One of Houston's latest and exhilarating activities. Imagine an incredible artificial climbing terrain that appears and feels like real rocks. This facility offers an extraordinary experience for any enthusiastic climber at any skill level; with a friendly staff of experts ready to assist you in every way. You will find this outfit to be clean, well run, and safety-minded. Here is where you go for that out-of-the-ordinary kind of family outing.

What an exciting place for birthday parties or any social activities, such as youth groups, scouts, or recreational groups. Be sure to make your reservation in advance, especially for evenings, weekends, and holidays.

Necessary climbing gear, including shoes and safety harnesses may be rented on-site. All climbers are required to pass a $3.75 Basic Safety Course.

Cost

Day Pass: $9.50   Harness Rental: $2   Shoe Rental: $3.50

Hours

Mon - Thur	Noon - 10 pm
Fri	Noon - 11 pm
Sat	10 am - 11 pm
Sun	10 am - 8 pm

Locker rooms with showers and restrooms are available along with a wonderful multi-purpose room that can accommodate any fun social activity. You may bring your own refreshments or ask the staff to arrange for pizza to be delivered.

Anyone is welcome to climb. However, I recommend that they be 6 years or older to enjoy this sport. Adult supervision is advised for children under 14 years of age. All people under 18 must have adult consent prior to climbing.

Directions

Take I-10 to Bunker Hill Road. Go north across railroad tracks. Turn left on Old Katy Road. Turn right at BKP Building and go 1 block to #102.

TEXAS STATE RAILROAD

Rusk, Texas
903-683-2561   or   800-442-8951

Take a ride on this vintage train

The rails were constructed over 100 years ago, in 1896. This railroad operated until 1969. Today, it is a living museum of railroad's golden age. The lines run 25 miles between Rusk and Palestine. Uses vintage steam engines built between 1890 and 1900. Board the train from either depot in Rusk or Palestine. This scenic trip takes four hours with an hour layover for lunch. Bring your own lunch, small coolers are allowed or lunch can be purchased at the depots. Offering sandwiches and barbecue. Also iced drinks and popcorn are sold on the train.

Opens mid-March until October. Train runs weekends only. However in June & July. it runs Thurs - Sun. The Train does not operate on Mondays, Tuesdays and Wednesdays. Call for times and to make reservations. Office hours are 8 to 5.

Cost

Children under 3 . . . . Free
Children ages 3-12 . . . . $9
Adults $15

Make reservations well in advance. At least 4 weeks ahead in the spring and 2 weeks in the summer/fall.

Directions

Depots located either at Rusk or at Palestine are approximately 150 miles from Houston. To get to the depot at Palestine, take I-45 North to Buffalo, then Highway 79 in to Palestine. Depot will be 3 miles east out of town on Highway 84. To get to the depot at Rusk, take 59 North to Lufkin, then Highway 69 North to Rusk. Depot will be 3 miles west out of town on Highway 84.

VIKING ARCHERY

9701 Honeywell
713-771-1281

Learn to shoot a bow and arrow

In business for over 36 years, Viking Archery's skilled professionals let you observe as they make bows and arrows. Only a few places in the world allow the public that opportunity. Interesting. Educational. Ask to go on a tour.

Their facility includes an air conditioned indoor range. Every Saturday at 10:30 am, families can enjoy learning how to shoot a bow and arrow in their archery class. Equipment—bows, arrows, and protective gear rent cheaply. On-hand instructors teach every thing you'll want to know about archery. Or practice shooting any time they're open.

Hours
Daily . . . . 10 am - 9 pm

Cost
Saturday morning lessons $5
Equipment rental $1.50
Practice $3/hr

Directions
From the Southwest Freeway, exit Bissonnett going south. Go right on Honeywell. (Will be 1 block east of the freeway.)

Locations

1. Adventure Outfitters
2. Alabama Bookstop
3. Antique Center of Texas
4. Burton's Antiques
5. Canoesport
6. City of Alvin's Antique Stores
7. Diho Market
8. Factory Outlet Malls
9. Favorite Shopping Areas
10. Fiesta Grocery Stores
11. Garden Ridge Pottery
12. Import Shops Along Harwin
13. Pottery Guild Shop
14. Trader's Village
15. Vintage Shops in Houston
16. Whole Earth Provisions

Chapter 9
UNIQUE PLACES TO SHOP

ADVENTURE OUTFITTERS

First Colony Mall
16539 Southwest Frwy Ste 550
Sugar Land TX 77479
281-265-2520
www.adventureoutfitters.com

An outdoor specialty store that also offers clinics, rentals, and travel advice for great family adventures

Besides carrying an extensive variety of recreational merchandise such as canoes, kayaks, climbing gear, camping and hiking equipment, maps and guide books, Adventure Outfitters gives you other ways of making family and group outings more exciting. They rent recreational equipment such as kayaks, backpacks, sleeping bags, and tents. Try out some of their popular equipment before you decide to purchase.

Adventure Outfitters also offers a variety of clinics free of charge. Their clinics on backpacking, climbing and camping are great for families as well as scout groups, school groups, and outdoor organizations.

Here you can get advice on unique experiences like weekend rock climbing trips. Or rafting & canoe trips for a few days to a week in the wilderness.

Hours
Mon - Sat . . . . 10 am - 9 pm
Sunday . . . . noon - 6 pm

Directions
Located in Sugar Land at the First Colony Mall next to J.C. Penny's and the Food Court. Take Hwy 59 South and exit Hwy 6.

ALABAMA BOOKSTOP BOOKSTORE

2922 South Shepherd
713-529-2345

Bookstore inside old movie theater

Nostalgia at its best. Many remember watching movies in the old Alabama Theater. Now it is Houston's largest bookstore.

Pay attention to the murals on the wall. Classical or New Age music adds to the unique atmosphere. Parking and entrance also in the rear.

Hours

Closed some holidays

Daily .... 9 am - Midnight

Directions

From the 59 Freeway, exit S.Shepherd/Greenbriar. Take South Shepherd north. (Street only goes north.) Go through two lights. Will be on the left. Located between Whole Foods Market and the Whole Earth Provisions.

ANTIQUE CENTER OF TEXAS

1001 West Loop North
713-688-4211

Texas' largest antique store

With the best collection of antique dealers in the state, this is any antique buff's dream. Over 200 dealers. Browse through their great selection of furniture, silver, gold, jewelry, glassware, crystal, collectibles, porcelain, paintings, toys, and china. And who knows what else you can find?

Hours

Daily .... 10 am - 6 pm

Plan to take your time. Restaurant on premises with excellent entree. Homemade desserts. A very clean, smoke-free, air conditioned facility.

Directions

Located 2 miles north of the Galleria on the Old Katy Road. From the 610 West Loop going north, exit Woodway/Memorial and stay on the feeder. Go two lights and turn left on Memorial/North Post Oak. (Be sure to stay in the right lane.) At the second light turn right on Old Katy Road. Watch for their sign.

BURTON'S ANTIQUES

9333 Harwin
713-977-5885 or 713-789-9363

Antique auction Friday and Monday nights

Here is where one can find treasures for a bargain. Come any Friday or Monday night when the auction begins. Public welcome. Recently, a friend bought an 1860s regulator clock in top condition for $100.

Hall trees, armoires, mirrors, beds, dressers. The list is long and everything goes to the highest bidder. View beforehand what will be auctioned. Some nights will be better.

Offering soft drinks, snacks, desserts. People are friendly and helpful. A fun thing to do.

Hours

Daily . . . . 9am - 5 pm

Closed Sunday

Auction Hours

Monday . . . . 7 pm
Friday . . . . 7 pm

Directions

Located on Harwin between Gessner and Fondren. From the Southwest Freeway, exit Fondren. Go north. Turn left on Harwin. Will be 1/4 mile on the left.

CANOESPORT

5808 S. Rice Avenue 77081
713-660-7000
www.canoesport.com

Heaven for any outdoor buff

It's their personalized service and quality equipment that make any outdoor adventure a great success.

You'll find high quality kayaks and canoes. Sign-up for lessons. Their expertise includes salt and freshwater fly fishing equipment and outdoor clothing, too. See what hi-tech does for the great outdoors. Most items in the store are manufactured with the latest technology.

Hours
Mon - Fri . . . . 10 am - 7 pm
Saturday . . . . 10 am - 4 pm

Directions
From the 610 West Loop south of the 59 Freeway, exit Fournace and go west to South Rice Avenue. Turn right. Will be one block on the left

CITY OF ALVIN'S ANTIQUE STORES
Alvin TX   281-331-0492
(Ask for map of area shops)

Alvin offers antiques
Becoming like Old Town Spring, you'll be surprised at the number of cute shops. Start by visiting:

Once Upon A Time Antiques
1004 E. Highway 6, Ph. 281-331-7676.
Located along Highway 6 South as you are driving (south) into Alvin. This restored old home is now a beautiful antique shop. Here you will find quality Victorian, American, and country antiques. Be sure to stop. The owner is a member of the local guild and can tell you where other antique stores are in the area. Brochure/map available.

Hours
Tues - Sat: 10:30 am - 5:30 pm / Sun: 12:30 pm - 5:30 pm

Dixieland Antiques
1255 W. Highway 6, 281-585-4085
Further down on Highway 6 South from Alvin is this beautiful shop with a huge mural painted along the outside. Filled with antique treasures. Hard to miss from the highway.

Hours
Mon - Sat . . . . 10 am - 5:30 pm

DIHO MARKET

9280 Bellaire
713-988-1881

Shop at this oriental grocery store

This isn't the only oriental grocery store in Houston but one of my favorites. Offering imported foods that make oriental dishes wonderful.

Find the items you need for that special dish or simply come and see what is new and unique. This is always a fun adventure. Educational. Great place to take the family.

Offering a good selection of fresh fish and seafood. I like buying their barbecue sauces or trying something new. Some items I have yet to discover what they are. I recommend a trip to this market.

Hours
Daily . . . . 9 am - 10 pm

Directions
*Located between the 59 Freeway and
the Sam Houston Tollway.*

FACTORY OUTLET MALLS
Houston has three factory outlet malls

The Houston area offers three fantastic factory outlet malls. Two are on the I-45 Freeway. One is in the Conroe area about one hour north of downtown. The other is located about 45 minutes south of downtown, near Webster. The I-10 mall is about one hour west of downtown in Sealy.

I. The Factory Outlet Mall on I-45 North
Prime Outlets, 11141 League Line Rd., 77303
409-756-0999

Representing different factories like Nike Shoes, Corning Ware, Naturalizer Shoes, Bass, L.A. Gear, and more. Will be 90 stores in all.

Directions: Located one hour from downtown Houston. Take I-45 north to the Conroe area. Take exit 91/League Line Road. You will see the Mall from the Freeway.

II. The Factory Outlet Mall on I-45 South
11001 Delaney Rd., LeMarc 77568
409-938-3333

Known as the **Lone Star State Factory Store.** Offering American Tourister, Famous Brands, Windsor T-shirt Company, Bugle Boy, Hathaway, Faberware, Perfumaria, Book Warehouse, and more. Ask at the information center for coupons.

Directions: Located 20 miles south of downtown Houston. Take I-45 South to Exit 13 (11001 Delany Road).

III. The Factory Outlet Mall on I-10 West
1402 Outlet Center Dr,, Sealy TX 77474
409-885-3200

Enjoy saving an average of 40% at the **Sealy Outlet Center.** Great place to go for back-to-school shopping.

Directions: Located 50 miles from Houston in Sealy , Texas. Take I-10 East to Exit 721. Make a u-turn under the freeway on to the east bound feeder road. The Outlet is on the south side of I-10.

FAVORITE SHOPPING AREAS

Highland Village Shopping Center: You'll find great places to lunch at the Highland Village Shopping Center: La Madeleine, Grotto, and Anthony's. Located at the 4000 block of Westheimer a few blocks east of the Galleria, the center features large selection of upscale shops.

The Montrose: Filled with offbeat antique shops, located on Westheimer from Woodhead to Mandell Streets. Watch for the Westheimer Street Festival held twice a year, with arts, crafts, and fun. 713-942-0800

River Oaks: Swanky shops. The first shopping district in Houston. The River Oaks Center, with art deco-inspired storefronts, offers more than 65 upscale stores located on West Gray. Favorites: River Oaks Theater (an art film cinema) and Tony Mandola's Gulf Coast Kitchen.

The Houston Heights: For antique-lovers. The Houston Heights offers some of the best antiquing in Houston. Best approach, from I-10, take either Heights Boulevard and Yale Street to 19th Street, where you will find the shops: The Heights Antiques Co-op, The Heights Pavilion, John's Flowers and Antiques, and Antiques on Nineteenth. While in the area, lunch at the local cafes or deli.

The Rice Village: A shopper's must-do. Near Rice University, this area buzzes with lots of unique little shops, about 325 of them. Lots of great places to lunch, too: Allegro Italian Bakery and Café, Trattoria Pasquale, Le Peep, Nit Nio (Thai) Prego, Calypso (Caribbean) La Madeleine, and the Croissant Brioche Café. Watch them make bagels at The Bagel Manufactory.

Upper Kirby District: Many art galleries locate between the Rice Village and River Oaks on Kirby. You'll find Gallery Row, with works from some of the best artists in Texas. This area offers lots of specialty and antiques shops, too.

FIESTA GROCERY STORES

6200 Bellaire
713-270-5889

Huge grocery stores specializing in international foods

Has a large selection of different foods to meet the needs of ethnic groups throughout the city. Very interesting grocery stores. Spend time browsing. Great place to go if you like cooking international dishes that require exotic ingredients.

These grocery stores cater to the ethnic neighborhoods in different areas of Houston, for example:

The store at 2300 North Shepherd

caters to Mexican foods.

The store at 8130 Kirby

carries a selection of Jewish foods..

The store at 1005 Blalock

has a large health food section.

The store at 6200 Bellaire

carries exotic foods for Asians, Africans, Mexicans, Indians, and more.

GARDEN RIDGE POTTERY

Three locations:

19411 Atrium Place, Houston
281-578-2334
(I-10 & Fry Road)

431 E. Airtex, Houston
281-821-7008
(I-45 North 2 1/2 miles north of Beltway 8. Take exit 62 and travel on the feeder to Airtex.)

12002 Southwest Freeway
281-240-4600
(In the City of Stafford)

Familiar to most of us but unique in that they started in Texas. Texan-style huge. Baskets, dried flowers, crafts items. That is just the start. Remember this place for those out-of-town guests.

Hours
Daily . . . . 9 am - 9 pm
Sunday . . . . 9 am - 7 pm

Unique Places  *To Shop*

IMPORT SHOPS
ALONG HARWIN BETWEEN GESSNER & FONDREN
Hundreds of shops along Harwin

You will find this a very interesting place to go shopping. Import shops supplied from merchandise brought in from the Houston ship channel.

You can find all kinds of things from silk plants, electronics, sports equipment, T-shirts, shoes, floor tiles, picture frames, handbags, clothing, toys, cosmetic items to leather goods. Much is at bargain prices.

Shops generally open at 10 am. Many shopkeepers speak only a little English.

Wear comfortable shoes. Plan to have plenty of time. Great place to go exploring. Make it an outing. I don't recommend bringing children along. Go with a friend.

Just around the corner on Gessner/Harwin is the Hong Kong Food Market. Worth a visit.

Directions
From the 59 Freeway, exit Fondren and go north to Harwin. Go left. Shops will be on both sides of the street.

POTTERY GUILD SHOP

2433 Rice Blvd
713-528-7687

Locals make pottery and sell in this unique shop

Handmade pottery crafted locally. Every piece is one-of-a-kind. Upstairs is extra gallery space. Be sure to see what's on hand.

Hours

Mon - Sat .... 10 am - 6 pm
Sunday .... 10 am - 4 pm

Directions

Located 1 block east of Kirby on Rice in the Rice University area. From the 59 Freeway, exit Kirby and go south. Turn left on Rice. Will be 3 shops past Kinko's.

TRADER'S VILLAGE
FLEA MARKET AND RV PARK
7979 N. Eldridge
281-890-5500

Huge flea market affair

Grand facility with spacious parking. Over 600 open-air booths offering a different variety every weekend. From puppies to furniture. A great place for crafts, antiques, hats, clothes, candles, leather goods, artwork and guns.

Hours
Sat & Sun ....7 am - 6 pm

Some weekends are better than others. Call ahead. Also events such as a swap meet, Indian powwow, a chili cook-off, a British car show and much more can add to the excitement. Parking is $2.

Directions
From the 610 West Loop, take Highway 290 eight miles to Eldridge Road. Go south 4 blocks.

Unique Places **To Shop**

VINTAGE SHOPS IN HOUSTON

"Timeless Taffeta"

1657 Westheimer   713-529-6299

Vintage clothing, costumes, wigs, leather clothing, new clothing, and more. Located between Shepherd and Montrose.

Hours

Mon - Sat	10:30 am - 7:30 pm
Sunday	Noon - 6 pm

"Wear It Again Sam"

1411 Westheimer   713-523-5258

Vintage clothing from the Victorian Age to the 70's. Old sunglasses, costumes, collectibles, lamps. Located between Montrose and Shepherd.

Hours

Mon - Sat	11 am - 6 pm
Sunday	1 pm - 5 pm

"Designer's Encore"

2296 Richmond   713-626-5235

Located on Richmond inside the 610 Loop. Designer clothes at bargain prices.

Hours

Mon - Fri	10 am - 6 pm
Saturday	10 am - 5 pm

River Oaks Closet Upscale Resale Shop

3502 S. Shepherd   713-522-0507
26620 Sage   713-526-2021

Hours

Tues - Sat	10 am - 6 pm

WHOLE EARTH PROVISIONS

2934 South Shepherd
713-526-5226

A mountain climbing gear store

Not only mountain climbing gear but lots of very new and innovative things. Want to plan a hiking or camping trip? Camping items. Canoes. You can find information and maps for almost anywhere in the world. A very entertaining place to shop.

Hours

Mon - Fri	....	10 am - 9 pm
Saturday	....	10 am - 6 pm
Sunday	....	Noon - 6 pm

Directions

Located next to the Whole Foods Market and the Alabama Bookstop. From the 59 Freeway, exit South Shepherd/Greenbriar. Take South Shepherd north. (Street only goes north.) Go through two lights. Will be on the left.

Other location: 6560 Woodway. 713-467-0234
Directions: Take Hwy 59 south and exit Fountainview. Turn right on Fountainview to woodway. Turn left on Woodway. It will be on your right.

Index

Index

Index

Index

Index

Index